The
Destination
of the Mirror

The
Destination
of the Mirror

A woman's quest to achieve with honesty as a companion

RUNGEEN SINGH

PARTRIDGE
A Penguin Random House Company

To order additional copies of this book, contact
Partridge India
000 800 10062 62
www.partridgepublishing.com/india
orders.india@partridgepublishing.com

DEDICATION

To my lovely mother Girja who got me educated
To my husband Yash who taught me courage
To my two sons Vikhyat and Sumraat
To my daughters-in-law Reena and Sonia
To my four exceptional grandsons
Shivang, Arhaan, Suryansh and Aarav
Who taught me the meaning of love
And full-filled my life with happiness

CHAPTER 1

Aina looked at her reflection in the mirror and smiled as she saw her husband Heera right behind her.

Heera said, "There is a special glow on your face today. Nobody can say that you are twenty six years old and that you are a mother of a two year old."

"It is because I am very happy. I have the best husband and the cutest daughter in the world. You are the breath of my life and Khushi is my heartbeat."

Heera said, "Actually this glow, I think, is also because life has finally sorted itself out for us."

It was a fact. Heera and Aina were more relaxed because Aina's traumatic marriage to Daman Rai had ended in a divorce, which was settled amicably, with an alimony of Rupees Two Hundred Thousand. Then both Heera and Aina had got married finally and their life seemed for the first time to be without obstacles.

"Yes Heera, and my cup is full, because I have found my real mother and my brother also. I always feel surprised when I think about my life. Was it just fate or some human factors, that today I am here with you? Just imagine! I could have been a dancing girl."

Aina had been brought up by her father Kalka and his wife Gomti, but then Aina had come to know that she was in reality, the daughter of the charming dancing girl Bijli, who had always been true to her father Kalka.

"Hush darling! Don't talk like this. Just think that your mother is a gem of a person. We all love her a lot."

"But it is the truth, Heera and we can't run away from the fact that my brother Laila is an eunuch."

Heera said, "He is your half brother, because he was born to your father and his wife Gomti."

"Do you feel embarrassed or humiliated because of Ma and Laila?"

"Never, Aina. For me they are great human beings and I respect them for that. Moreover Laila is a wonderful brother and he is so caring and loving."

"You are caring and loving also. What a co-incidence that I had to meet you through my first husband Daman Rai because you were working for him."

"Very true! If you had not been married to Daman, I would not have met you and we would not have fallen in love. So we should be thankful to Daman for providing us the opportunity to meet."

"Specially as even now in 1964, love marriages are not appreciated so much by society. Well, you are great and very brave, husband dear. You have married a divorcee like me and you have accepted an eunuch and a dancing girl in your family. All these are unacceptable to the society nowadays. You have a very large heart."

"God forbid. A large heart would mean a diseased heart. No, Aina. I have done nothing special. You, your mother and brother are great human beings and I respect human beings who are true and honest and who have integrity, loyalty and sincerity."

They heard their baby daughter Khushi crying and both of them started fussing over the baby, but Khushi went on crying. She just wouldn't stop.

Heera said, "Let me put on the radio. Khushi loves to hear the songs on Vividh Bharti radio station."

As Heera started tuning the radio to the required radio station, the radio caught the news on All India Radio. Heera was about to change the station, when he heard the news headlines, and his hand stopped at once.

The impersonal voice of the newsreader was saying, "The spy Rocoo has escaped from the jail. The police have put up a massive search for Rocoo."

Another news item followed, but Heera and Aina were not listening. Heera was looking at Aina with real concern. It seemed that Khushi too had understood the gravity of the situation as she stopped crying.

Rocoo had been tried and found guilty of spying. He had been sentenced for fourteen years.

Aina said, "Heera, what will happen now? This is bad news for us."

Heera said, "What do you think Rocoo will do?"

Aina agreed, "Rocoo will definitely want to take revenge, because he knows that I am responsible for getting him caught, and also because I gave testimony in his case. He used to glare at me in court also. He will not spare me. He will be after my blood."

"He knows that we live here in this house. Do you want us to shift from this house?" asked Heera.

"No Heera. We can't run away just because an enemy spy wants to take revenge. It would be cowardly."

Heera nodded and added, "Your ex-husband Daman Rai is also in danger from Rocoo."

Aina replied, "Yes, in court Rocoo had shouted at both Daman and me, 'I will get even with both of you.' Daman Rai will certainly be on his radar."

Heera said, "I think we can follow that adage, 'Discretion is the better part of valour'. If you want, we can leave Rojpur and go and live in some other city."

A rough voice snarled, "It is already too late."

Startled, Heera and Aina swirled round to see Rocoo standing with a gun pointed at Aina.

Heera was about to pounce on Rocoo, but he anticipated it, and said, "Heera, don't act smart with me, otherwise I will blow out the brains of your baby."

"What do you want?" asked Heera.

"I want to kill you and your wife."

Aina said, "What are you waiting for? Kill us. We are not stopping you. Why aren't you killing us?"

Rocoo said, "Because you Madam, have to do a small thing for me. You have to go to the police and tell them the story I tell you. It will be slightly different from the evidence you gave in court"

"Why would the police believe me?" asked Aina.

Rocoo answered, "It is for you to be convincing. See, you told the court that I am the culprit. Now you have to say that Daman Rai had forced you and me at gun point to say and act as we did."

Aina said, "I won't do it."

Rocoo hissed, "You don't have any soft feelings for Daman Rai, so why are you refusing?"

Aina replied, "Because your plan is full of holes."

Heera said, "She is right, the police will not buy it. And why do you want to involve her? Uselessly she will get embroiled. I will not let her do this."

Rocoo snarled, "Heera, look at your wife and daughter. They are alive and well. Would you prefer to see their dead bodies?"

Heera did not answer, and Rocoo pointed the gun at their baby Khushi, saying, "Decide quickly."

CHAPTER 2

Heera looked at Aina and saw the helplessness on her face. His mind whirled, trying to find a way out. He quickly thought of ways that they could use to evade Rocoo, but no idea came to him.

Finally Heera said, "No, I would not like to see them dead. I want them alive and free from danger."

Rocoo said, "Then tell your wife that she has to go to the police station."

Heera said, "Let my wife remain here with the baby. I will go and talk to the police."

"What will you do in the police station?"

"I will tell them that her life is in danger because Daman Rai has threatened her. I will also tell the police that Daman also forced you, so you should be spared."

Rocoo snarled, "Very funny! Heera, do you think that I am stupid? Your wife was the one who gave the evidence, so the police will listen to her and not to you. She has to go to the police."

"Rocoo, she has to look after a baby, how can she go to a police station?"

"Heera, how did she manage to go to the court to give evidence against me?"

Heera said, "We had her mother and brother here to baby sit, but they have gone out of station. Now there is no one to take care of the baby."

Rocoo replied, "I will look after the baby. Give the baby to me and let us go to the police."

Rocoo started walking towards Aina who had Khushi in her arms. With one hand holding the gun, Rocoo extended his other arm to take the baby.

Aina said firmly, "Rocoo, don't you dare touch my baby. I will not give my baby to you, come what may. You may shoot us, but then you will lose the only opportunity you have, of becoming free. We may think of helping you, but only if you stay away from my baby."

Rocoo stared at Aina and she glared right back at Rocoo unflinchingly. Then his eyes wavered because he knew that only Aina could help him by going to the police, so he had to toe her line.

Suddenly, Heera lunged towards Aina, grabbed her and rushed towards the inner door, but Rocoo was quick. Rocoo ran and stood between them and the door, saying, "Not so fast! Don't play tricks with me. I might just shoot you three. I am running out of patience."

Aina knew that Rocoo meant business. He would let them be alive, only till he felt that she would go to the police and say what he wanted her to say, so Aina spoke in a resigned manner, "All right, give me the details of your plan. What should I tell them? Will you come with us to talk to the police officer?"

"Ofcourse not! They will arrest me at once. Don't you know that I have run away from their custody? I will stand outside the police station, with my gun pointing at you. And if you think that you can say what you want and incriminate me, let me tell you, I have my man inside. He will hear whatever you say and he will keep an eye on you. If you do not act as planned, he will signal to me and I will shoot you three."

"All right, let us go," said Heera.

"Not now. Let it be a little dark, then we will go. Give me something to eat. I am famished," said Rocoo.

Heera commented caustically, "I forgot that I had sent you an invitation to attend a party here."

Rocoo just walked to the side table where some bananas were kept. He picked them up and still with the gun in his hand, he started peeling them and eating them. He ate all dozen of them.

Heera and Aina watched him like hawks, waiting for the slightest drop of his attention, to try and escape. Khushi started crying because she was hungry and Aina started walking into the inner room.

Rocoo shouted, "Stay here. Don't move."

Heera replied firmly, "She has to feed the baby. She has to go inside that room. You can check that room. There is no outer door to escape. Moreover I am standing right here as a hostage. Aina cannot and will not run away anywhere."

Aina resolutely walked into the inner room. As she fed Khushi, she looked around the room trying to think of ideas to escape, but it was a room with only one window which was barred by a metal grill. She quickly picked up a pen and paper, when Rocoo started shouting for her to come out.

She walked out, sat down on a chair and burped the baby. It was still sunny outside and they had to wait for some more time. Heera signalled to Aina that Rocoo was sleepy. Then they waited for Rocoo to doze off, but seated on a chair, Rocoo kept fighting his sleep.

Finally Rocoo stood up and started pacing about the room. With the dip in the sunlight, he rasped out, "Come on. Let us go. I will be right behind you and if you do anything, I will shoot you three first and think later. Now, just move out."

Heera took Khushi in his arms and with Aina, he walked out of their house. Rocoo followed them and after Heera had locked the door, Rocoo snatched the house keys from his hand. Then he made Heera and Aina walk towards the police station. He followed right behind them, often digging the gun into Heera's back, specially when people walked near them.

Slowly the sunlight was fading into dusk and it was difficult to make out faces. Rocoo then forced them till the police station steps and prodded them to go in. As they were about to climb the steps, suddenly Rocoo snatched Khushi from Heera's arms and ran away.

Aina and Heera were about to run after him, when they heard his voice say sharply, "Better go inside the police station, if you want the child alive."

They had no option but to obey. Slowly Heera and Aina went inside. They were taken to the Police Inspector and made to wait. After that, Heera could see Rocoo's face peering from the window and he could also see the glint of the gun on the window sill outside.

CHAPTER 3

After waiting for some time, they were called to meet the Inspector, who looked up at them and said, "Yes, I am Inspector Verma. What can I do for you?"

Verma was sitting with his back to the window and thus Aina and Heera had to sit facing the window. They realized that Rocoo could hear whatever was being said, because the window was open. There was a metal grill, but it had space enough for a gun to point at them.

Heera said, "Inspector, we have come regarding the case of the trial of Rocoo as a spy."

Verma sat up and said, "He escaped from the jail recently. We are looking out for him. Do you know anything about where Rocoo is?"

Heera said, "She is my wife, Aina. She had given the testimony in that case."

"I read all that because now I am working on Rocoo's case," said Verma impatiently.

Aina said, "I want to change my testimony."

"Where is Rocoo?" asked Inspector Verma.

"I want to say that I had been threatened and therefore I had said what I did," said Aina.

"First tell me if you know where Rocoo is," insisted Inspector Verma.

Heera felt desperate and he kicked Verma under the table. Verma looked under the table angrily. Aina had written DANGER on the paper she had brought from her room. She had thrown it down. The anger of Verma changed to consternation when he saw the paper. He realized that something was amiss, so he said, "I will have to write down whatever you have to say."

He rose and started fussing around with the files and registers on his table. Unobtrusively, Aina scribbled, "Rocoo outside the window with my baby."

Verma saw her writing something. He dropped a file as if by accident and Aina bent to pick it up. She gave him the file and the paper on which she had written. Inspector Verma kept the file on the table.

Much to his credit, he did not bat an eyelid to show that Aina had given him some information. He just said in a matter of fact tone, "The register is not here. I will just get it. You both wait a second."

Aina said, "Atleast hear what we have to say. I have to go to my baby. She is very small."

Inspector Verma said in a clipped tone, "You should have left your baby in safe hands. We cannot help it. We have a protocol to follow, Madam," and then he winked at Heera and Aina, who also sat with impassive faces without reacting. But actually Aina and Heera were beside themselves with worry. Their Khushi was in the hands of a cold blooded spy, and they couldn't do anything about it. Both wished that the police would not do anything that would risk their baby's life.

Inspector Verma went away to the other room, asking for the register in a loud voice. Then after a couple of minutes, he returned and sat down at his table.

Soon they heard the sound of a scuffle outside the window. After that they heard a shot being fired.

Aina screamed as she was suddenly afraid for Khushi. "Has he shot her?" she whimpered.

Just then a policeman came in and he said, "We nearly caught Rocoo, but he managed to run away."

"Was anybody hit by the shot?" asked Heera.

"We don't know. It is very dark outside."

"The baby! Where is my baby?" gasped Aina.

"He must have taken the baby as we didn't see the baby anywhere," answered the policeman.

They rushed outside. It was extremely dark and they could not see anything, except the light coming from a room of the police station.

Aina and Heera started looking around like they both had gone beserk. Verma hissed out sharply to them, "Rocoo may still be around here. He may shoot at you, so be careful."

"I don't care. I have to find my baby," replied Heera, as he and Aina frantically started looking in the bushes which they could see from the light of the room.

At that moment, the clouds moved away and the moon shone in the sky. In the moonlight, they could now see the bushes on the right of the police station.

Suddenly, Verma shouted, "Blood! There is a trail of blood here through the bushes. That means Rocoo was hit by the shot. Let us follow this trail. Both of you better stay here. It is dangerous, because if Rocoo has been hit, then he will be sure to shoot at us."

Perforce, Heera and Aina had to stop. They looked around but could not see Khushi.

Heera suddenly said, "Aina, what is that white cloth under the tree?"

They rushed towards it and picked up the white cloth. Aina said, "It is the sheet in which I had wrapped

Khushi. Oh Heera! It has blood on it. Does that mean that Khushi has been shot?"

"Aina, that blood does not prove anything. The blood could be Rocoo's blood. Maybe Rocoo has left Khushi here and she is some where close."

They started looking for Khushi with demented desperation and they were just about to give up their search, when they heard a sound of a cry.

Heera shouted, "Khushi's cry! Oh! That means she is alive!" They looked around to locate where their baby was. The cries gained momentum and they followed the sound till they reached the tree. And then they saw Khushi in a deep hole in the trunk of the tree.

They picked up Khushi and first checked her. They found that she had no injury and that she was safe. They then lavished their relief and love on their bundle of joy for some time, and then it was time to think.

Aina asked, "Heera, what should we do now?"

"If Rocoo is caught, then we will be safe."

"But Heera, if Rocoo is not caught, then Rocoo can come again and even kill us, as he must be mad with us, for telling the police about him."

"Aina, let us go inside the police station and wait till we get to know about Rocoo, then we can decide our next step. One thing is certain. Now Rocoo will definitely be after our blood. Let us hope for the best."

.

CHAPTER 4

Heera and Aina kept sitting in Inspector Verma's office. They knew that Rocoo had his man in the office, so they conversed in whispers. Heera whispered, "Aina, whether Rocoo is caught or not, we should leave this city and go away to live in some other city. If he is caught, he himself will trouble us. If he is not caught, his people will be after us. I can't take a chance with you and Khushi."

"Heera, won't that be a cowardly thing to do?"

"It is better to show a clean pair of heels sometimes, and this is a very dangerous time for us. We have a duty to give a safe and secure life to Khushi."

"But Heera, what about your job? You will have to leave your job and look for another job. Till you get another job, how will we manage financially? I don't want to touch the money kept in Khushi's name. That money is for her. I don't want her to suffer when she grows up."

Heera said, "I agree totally. But I have my savings and that will see us through till I get a job."

"Where can we go?"

"It depends on where I can get a job."

Just then Inspector Verma came back and said, "Sorry folks. Rocoo got away, but he has certainly been shot. We will now check on all the hospitals because he must need medical care." He called his subordinate to check in all the hospitals and clinics.

Heera intervened, "Rocoo has the keys of our house. I am sure he must be in my house. Did you check there?" Heera told Verma the location of their house.

Verma said, "We didn't go that side, because the trail of blood was in the opposite direction."

"He must have done it purposely to throw you off his trail," said Heera.

Verma got up and said, "We will check your house. Till then you stay here."

Before going to Heera's house Verma instructed his peon to get tea and snacks for Aina and Heera.

Heera was proved right. Rocoo had gone to their house. He had opened the lock and bolted the door from inside, and he had tried to wash his wound. He had fallen asleep out of exhaustion and loss of blood, and when Inspector Verma had reached the house, they had broken the panes of a window, opened the window and jumped into the house. They had found Rocoo sleeping inside. He had tried to resist, but in vain, as soon he was surrounded and overpowered by the police. Rocoo was thus caught by Inspector Verma and his policemen.

Rocoo looked pale when he was brought inside the police station. His eyes were livid as they glared at Heera and Aina, and he said, "I will get even with you both soon. I have made arrangements for that. You disrupted my life, now I will not let you live peacefully."

Rocoo was put behind bars, and Aina and Heera came back home with Khushi. The next day, the newspapers were full of the heroic efforts of the police in catching Rocoo again. Aina and Heera were thankful that their names were not at all mentioned in the news reports. Then Heera said, "I am so glad that Rocoo is behind bars. There is something sinister about him."

"But what could Rocoo have meant when he said that he had made arrangements for getting even with us? Maybe we should move away from Rojpur. Rocoo may try and get someone to hurt Khushi."

"I also think so, Aina. We will work something out. Just now I have to go to office. If I didn't have to withdraw my salary, I wouldn't have gone."

"Don't worry about me, Heera. I will manage alone and I will be very alert."

Heera left for his office and Aina became busy with her household chores. She collected the glass pieces of the broken window and made a mental note that it had to be fixed as soon as possible, because it could be a security hazard, as anyone could come in.

And that is exactly what happened. Aina had just put Khushi to sleep when she felt that someone was in the room behind her. She looked around and screamed when she saw a burly man with long moustaches standing behind her. He clamped his hand on her mouth and said in an ominous voice, "Keep quiet. I have a gun. You have troubled us enough. Now it is the end for you."

"Who are you?" asked Aina.

"Oh! So you want me to introduce myself? I am Rocoo's colleague Maakhan and you are my enemy, because you twice got Rocoo behind bars."

"What do you want?"

"I want two things. First I want you, because you are quite beautiful. Secondly I want to kill you because that is the order I have got from Rocoo."

"What will Rocoo gain from having me killed?"

"Satisfaction of a revenge well taken! Actually he didn't want you killed. He wanted that you should get him free from the spy case, but you never obey. So now he wants you killed. So first things first, I will satisfy my thirst," said Maakhan, and he grabbed Aina.

Despite the revulsion she was feeling, Aina let him crush her to his huge body and then she fluttered her eyes and said, "Oh my! What a strong body you have! So unlike my lean husband. I have often told him to build up his muscles, but he never listens to me. I am quite disgusted with him."

"Really?" Maakhan looked at her with surprise and then with one hand he pulled the mattress that was lying in a corner and lay it on the floor. He tried to drag Aina and she suddenly pouted, "Why are you in such a hurry? Why can't you let me enjoy everything?"

"What? Do you actually want it?"

"How stupid you are! Is this something I will admit? No woman will admit to it, however much she wants it. Now listen. We have all the time in the world. My husband has gone to the office and he will come back in the evening. Have you eaten anything?"

"No. I had no time to eat," said Maakhan, a trifle mollified by her alluring stance.

"Now let me feed you first. Bring a plate and sit down on the mat. I have potatoes ready and now I will fry some puris for you. Eat this. Then we will have fun."

Completely taken in by her sweet talk, Maakhan sat down and she filled his plate with potatoes and hot puris which she was frying in hot oil. As he became busy in eating, Aina started throwing spoonfuls of burning oil at him. Soon he was howling at the top of his voice.

Aina ran and picked up Khushi. Then she went and stood outside, where her neighbours had already come up to see what the hollering was about. When they understood what had happened, they caught Maakhan and handed him to the police. Inspector Verma came and complimented Aina, "Madam, you are really brave. You showed very good presence of mind. I salute you."

Aina went to a shop to telephone Heera and he came home at once, then he came to know what had happened with Aina. Heera became serious. He said, "We must leave Rojpur and go away to some other city."

"Where can we go, Heera?"

"I talked to people in my office and they were saying that Kanpur would have more job opportunities than Lucknow, because Kanpur has more industries. I am not taking any chances by staying on here in Rojpur. Rocoo might have put other people against us. Let us go to Kanpur at once. Now we must start packing."

Aina walked to the window and looked outside in the fading light for a long time. Heera came and asked, "What is the matter, Aina? What are you looking at?"

"I have this uncanny feeling that someone is watching us."

Heera said gravely, "All the more reason for us to leave Rojpur. I am going to get the window glass pane repaired, so that no one can come into our house."

"Heera, please be careful," implored Aina.

"You go into the inner room and bolt the door from inside, as anyone can come through this broken pane. Open your door only when you hear my voice."

When he was sure that Aina and Khushi were in the inner room and Aina had bolted the door from inside, Heera got the man to repair the window glass pane, and then he came and told Aina to unbolt the door.

CHAPTER 5

As Heera owned his house, so he decided to just lock it and go. He thought that later on he would come back and sell the house. As they had to arrange a lot of things, they quickly planned what they had to do.

Heera and Aina decided that they would carry all their money with them. He took out the alimony money of Rupees Two Hundred Thousand and his own savings of Rupees One Hundred Thousand from the bank. They knew that they were taking a risk by carrying so much money, but there was no other way, because Heera did not know when he would be able to return to Rojpur.

Aina sat down and made a list of things that would be needed for setting up a new household in Kanpur. Then she started packing the necessities which she could carry easily in two trunks. She kept all the things that Khushi could need.

Suddenly, there was a knock at the door. Heera looked through the window and was shocked to see Aina's ex-husband Daman Rai standing outside. Heera was confused whether he should open the door to let him in. Daman and Aina had been divorced and Daman had already given alimony to Aina, so why was Daman standing outside their front door? Would Aina like it?

Heera did not realize that Aina was standing near him already and she had seen Daman.

She said, "Let him come in, otherwise I will die of curiosity as to why he came to meet us. Don't worry. He can't harm us any more and now he has no effect on me. I am not afraid of him anymore."

Heera opened the door and Daman walked in. He looked at them and said, "I read the news that Rocoo had escaped from the jail. I tried to find out the progress from the police, but they didn't tell me anything."

Aina and Heera kept quiet and Daman Rai continued, "I realized that Aina, you may know, as you gave testimony against Rocoo. If he has escaped, he would come to you first, because I know that he is a vindictive man. Do you know anything about Rocoo?"

Heera looked at Aina and she nodded her head, and Heera told Daman, "Yes, Rocoo had come here and he wanted Aina to go and tell the police, that at gunpoint, you had made Aina and Rocoo tell lies."

"Me? But he was the spy," exclaimed Daman.

Heera continued, "He wanted Aina to convince the police that you were responsible and you were the spy, not Rocoo. He took our baby and we went to the police and, to cut a long story short, Rocoo has been caught and is in police custody again."

The relief on Daman's face was apparent to both of them, but he stiffened as Heera said, "But the danger is still there. Rocoo has told his men to take revenge from Aina. So he may have told his men to take revenge from you too, Daman."

"How do you know that he has told his people to take revenge from Aina?"

"Because one of his men came here and tried to kill Aina, but she was too clever for him. She showed him as if he was welcome, but then she threw spoonfuls of hot oil on him and Maakhan's screams got the neighbours to catch him and hand him to the police."

"What did you say the name was? Maakhan? Was he a burly man with long moustaches?"

"Yes, but why are you looking so upset?"

"Heera, Maakhan is working for me. Oh Lord! He could have killed me any time."

Aina said, "You should think why he didn't kill you till now."

Daman scowled at her, "Are you being sarcastic?"

Aina replied, "No. I am only saying that if he hasn't killed you, he might be playing for higher stakes."

Daman asked, "You may be right. Do you know where he is?"

Aina said, "The neighbours had handed him over to the police. After that we don't know what happened to him. Didn't he contact you?"

Daman said, "No, he has not contacted me. He had taken leave, so I didn't even expect him to contact me. But I wonder what Maakhan wants from me."

Heera stated, "I guess now Maakhan will be used by Rocoo to make you say that you are the spy, and you forced Rocoo to take the blame. Rocoo is planning this so that he can be freed."

Daman said, "So there is danger that they will blackmail me into taking Rocoo's blame on my head. That means they will not kill me yet. So for the time being my life is safe. Now I have to see whether Maakhan comes back to work for me or not."

Heera said, "He will take time because he was badly burnt. Excuse me Daman, but we are in a hurry. We have a lot to do."

"You are packing your luggage. And that is a lot of luggage. Where are you going?" asked Daman.

"Away from this city," said Aina.

"Are you going permanently? Where are you going?" Daman seemed very curious.

"We don't know yet. We will go wherever our destiny takes us."

Daman said, "I don't care what happens to you both, as you both have troubled me such a lot. Needless to say, it is good riddance from my side. I will not miss you both at all. I hope I never have to see your faces."

"You weren't good to us either. Rather you were extremely cruel and nasty towards my wife. So it is good riddance from our side too. We will not miss you either. I hope we never meet again."

Daman went away and Heera and Aina got busy with the packing of their stuff.

CHAPTER 6

Very early in the morning, Aina asked, "Heera, have you kept the money safely?"

"Yes. Don't worry about it. I have a secret pocket in my vest. I have kept it all there. It is safe," said Heera.

Soon Heera and Aina with Khushi were sitting in a tonga (horse carriage) and proceeding to the railway station.

Aina said, "Are you sure no one is following us? I am still feeling as if something ominous will happen."

Heera consoled her, "We have taken all the precautions that we could. We sat on this tonga away from our house. We took our luggage surreptiously. Khushi also did not cry even once. I think that no one could have realized that we are going."

Suddenly Aina pointed at the tonga driver. Heera said, "He is a person I know. I have been using his tonga regularly for conveyance. He is trustworthy. That is why I told him in the evening to come to take us to the station early in the morning. And see he has come. Now relax, Aina."

Aina asked, "Heera, shouldn't we tell Verma that we are leaving Rojpur and going to Kanpur?"

"That may not be a good idea. He might tell other people and somehow Rocoo may get to know it. Rocoo even said that he has a man in the police station. We shouldn't tell anyone. When I come back to sell the house, then I will meet Verma and tell him the details. We mustn't talk to anyone on the train even, so be careful," cautioned Heera.

"There is a tonga coming behind us. Besides the tonga driver, there is only one passenger and that passenger has a grey sheet draped around his shoulders. I have seen this man somewhere."

"You are right, Aina. The figure does look familiar. Oh! He is the beggar man who used to sit at the corner of our lane. Oh dear! Was he spying on us? Let us check whether he is really following us."

Then Heera told the tonga driver to slow down, the other tonga also slowed down. Heera told the tonga driver to go faster and the other tonga also was made to go faster. The tonga driver said, "That tonga has been chasing us since we started. Maybe they want to ambush you and steal your stuff."

Heera replied, "The tonga is certainly chasing us. Do you know the beggar man who used to sit at the corner of our lane?"

"Sir, I had never seen him before, but he has been sitting there regularly for the past ten days."

Heera remarked, "He must have been spying on us."

"So you are in danger. Don't worry. You have been very kind to me always. You have given me extra money many times. Now I will get you away from this tonga. Just hold tightly."

The tonga driver got the horse into a gallop and soon they were hurtling down the road. Aina held on to the tonga with one hand and held Khushi with the other. Heera held Aina with one hand and the tonga with the other. They looked behind and saw that the other tonga was coming fast, but gradually it was obvious that its horse was weak and undernourished, while the horse of their tonga was stronger, and their tonga driver was putting all his stamina in saving them.

The other tonga was gradually left far behind. Soon they reached the railway station. The tonga driver helped them with the luggage and Heera paid him generously and thanked him for saving them.

The tonga driver said, "Go fast, Sir, before the other tonga comes. If they don't see you, they might think that you have gone to the bus station."

They ran inside and luckily, there was a train for Kanpur within an hour. They went to buy tickets for Kanpur. Heera made Aina stand in the queue, because the shorter queue for ladies would get tickets faster. Aina was able to get tickets for the unreserved compartment and they ran to the platform. Aina kept looking behind her, still afraid that someone might be tailing them.

Both Heera and Aina were impatient for the train to arrive, because they had started feeling that it was risky for them to stay on at Rojpur. Aina covered her face and Heera threw a sheet around his shoulders just to camouflage themselves, and they both kept a look-out for the beggar man.

Finally the train arrived and then they forgot the beggar man because it was a fight to get into the unreserved compartment. People were jamming the door and there was so much pushing and pulling, that Aina had a tough time keeping Khushi free from the jostling crowd.

A couple with seven children made matters worse. The husband first shoved his fat wife into the door of the compartment. Then he put his children inside the compartment one by one through the window. Then their numerous pieces of luggage were thrown inside through the window by the husband. Then he himself elbowed everyone out, to get inside the compartment.

By the time Aina and Heera managed to get into the compartment, with all their luggage, the berths were jam packed. Finally Heera and Aina had to sit in the aisle, on their metal trunks. Later Aina got to sit on the berth, but it was a wooden berth without cushions, which was as uncomfortable as the metal trunk.

Heera kept checking the money he had kept in the pocket of his vest, because there usually were many pickpockets who would use the crowded places more for picking pockets. Apart from this tension, there were many more problems in the unreserved compartment.

It was a frightful journey with passengers packed like the proverbial sardines, and the children screaming from lack of space. People were carrying breakable earthen containers to carry water. Many of them broke, and water got spilled all over the compartment. So the compartment soon became dirty.

Moreover the fans were not working and it soon became unbearably hot and stuffy. If anyone had to go to the stinky toilet, they had to literally walk over the others. Aina had an extra sensitive nose, so all this troubled her more. Heera and Aina had a more taxing railway journey because Khushi kept crying.

Aina made a mental note that she would never travel in an unreserved compartment again.

CHAPTER 7

They finally reached Kanpur and went on a tonga to the nearest lodge that the tonga driver knew about. The tonga plied through narrow lanes, over populated by not only human beings, but also cows and street dogs.

Aina commented, "The roads are so congested."

The tonga driver said, "Kanpur is an industrial town, so people come to get jobs from the neighbouring villages. That is why Kanpur is so congested."

Aina said, "In comparison Najapur and Rojpur are such quiet towns."

The tonga driver said, "How do you know about Najapur and Rojpur?"

"My ancestral house is in Najapur," replied Aina.

"And I stayed in Rojpur," said Heera.

"What a co-incidence! I am from Rojpur. Have you come here for a short stay or to get a job?"

"I have come to get a job and stay here permanently. How can I go about it?"

"Don't you worry. Now that you are from my town, I will take you to the best lodge."

"How can I get accommodation on rent?"

The tonga driver said, "I can help you in that. There are three rooms that are vacant near the River Ganga. My brother Naren stays there. He is working in a factory nearby. Maybe he can get you a job too."

"How lucky we are to have met you. What is your name?" asked Aina.

The tonga driver said, "My name is Rajan. But I will say one thing. Be alert. Don't trust anyone here. You both look so simple and honest, that people may cheat you. You must be clever enough to protect your own interests. Here, now we have reached our destination. This is the best lodge in the city. Stay here and tomorrow I will come and tell you about your accommodation."

They found the lodge quite a decent place to stay in. Next day Rajan came on his tonga and said, "I have found out that those three rooms near the Ganga are still vacant. You can come with me and see them."

They immediately went with Rajan on his tonga and they had a tough time. Aina was holding onto Khushi and Heera was holding Aina tightly, because Rajan took the tonga fast through the unruly surging traffic. Aina and Heera went on repeating, "Slow down please. Take it easy," but Rajan replied, "This is the only way to get some where in this busy traffic."

Finally they reached a more quiet area. Here the roads were less congested and the area appeared neater and more beautiful. Then Rajan took them to a cluster of houses which Aina found delightful. They got down and were thrilled that they could see the River Ganga from there. They found the three rooms suitable too. As the house was vacant, they could rent it at once.

Heera said, "We will take these three rooms."

The next day they shifted into the new house.

"I was meaning to ask you one thing. Why have you taken a house with three rooms?" asked Aina, as they kept their luggage inside the largest room.

"Because your mother and brother will stay with us. They will need a room and there should be a room for Khushi." Aina was very touched that without her saying anything, Heera had already thought of calling her mother Bijli and her brother Laila.

She said, "Thank you, Heera. You are really a very wonderful person. I respect you a lot as you are not afraid that people may taunt you about Ma and Laila."

"Oh dear me! Respect!? Lady, I want your love. Now I think we should have a private celebration in our new house to really make it a lovely home?"

"Yes ofcourse. I will make a special dinner with all your favourite dishes."

"No Lady. That won't do. I have other delectable imaginative ideas to make it really special."

Despite shy reluctance from Aina, that is exactly what Heera did. Throughout the evening, Heera wooed her with sweet words and caresses and when Khushi slept, the natural progression was that the only sound that could be heard to break the quietude of the night, was the melodious jingling of bangles, first with mellow love and then with ardent passion.

The next morning Aina was cooking breakfast. She was sitting on the floor and making tea on the stove, when she felt that someone was looking at her. As she looked up, she got the start of her life. She was looking straight into the near-human inquisitive eyes of a monkey who had come into the room through the open door. And the monkey was fat and totally in command. A loaf of bread lay between Aina and the monkey.

Aina was too paralysed with fright to do or say anything. Slowly, and with studied determination, the monkey picked up two slices, then two more, then more and more, till only two slices were left. By that time, Aina had composed herself enough to shout 'dhut dhut' at the monkey who returned the compliment with a 'khao khao'.

Aina shouted, "Heera, help me." The monkey seemed to look at her reproachfully and then, with great dignity the monkey walked off, looking back pityingly at the petrified Aina. Heera came in to see the monkey sitting outside on the boundary wall, coolly eating the bread slices. Aina shrieked, "The impudence of that monkey! See, it is laughing at me."

Heera burst out laughing and he said, "You must say that the monkey is very considerate. See, he knows we are two people here who eat bread, so he has left just two slices for us."

"It is not funny. I was terrified to see him so close to me."

"Aina, you are so beautiful, that even monkeys can't resist you." Aina ran after Heera to hit him playfully and they convulsed with laughter. Heera heard Aina laughing uproariously and he just stared at her.

It was good to see her laughing. Life had been so traumatic that they hadn't been able to have fun. He promised to himself that he would make sure that now there would be laughter in their house always.

The first thing that Heera did was to open a bank account and keep all the money in the bank. Gradually Aina and Heera settled down in their rented house also. They bought only the basic necessities because they wanted to conserve their money. Aina wanted that they should just buy mattresses and sleep on the floor, but Heera insisted that they buy two jute cots which they put in the bigger room.

Aina had brought a few inexpensive sheets from Rojpur and she put them up as curtains. In the other rooms, Aina just put mattresses and nothing else. The room was left free for Khushi so that she could be safe while Aina was busy with her household chores, as Aina had decided that she would not keep any servant.

When everything was complete, Heera looked around happily and said, "Aina, you certainly know how to make a house with four walls look like a home."

Khushi too seemed to be happy with her surroundings because she did not become irritable. She would walk with uncertain steps, and play with the toys that Aina would leave for her. From the window of her room, she loved watching the pigeons who frequented the courtyard.

Though he often went to look for a job, Heera gave a lot of time and attention to Khushi. It was a heartwarming sight for Aina to see Khushi gurgling, as Heera played with her. Soon everything seemed to settle down except that Heera did not get a job. But they had been prepared for that. There was no immediate financial crunch because they had Heera's savings to bank upon. What was unsettling was that Aina started getting nightmares again.

CHAPTER 8

One night she dreamt about herself. "Aina saw herself as a skinny dark girl, standing and crying. All her siblings were playing on the huge terrace, but she was lonely and she hated being lonely. Suddenly she heard weird sounds of 'huuuaaa huuaaa'. She looked up at the sky and she saw numerous pigeons flying up and then swooping down on another flock of pigeons, before returning to the terrace from where they had flown in the first place. She felt like flying like the pigeons in the sky, not alone, never alone, but in a group. Suddenly she saw a pigeon coming to attack her and its face became the face of a man, who said, "I have come to take Khushi." She shouted, "Save her. He will kill Khushi". And it was Rocoo's face. "Save Khushi," shouted Aina and she screamed." Heera woke up and held her like a child, gently talking to her, "Khushi is safe, Aina. You are dreaming. Go to sleep again." Aina went to sleep.

The nightmare came back. "Then Aina heard her mother's voice. She started moving at once. Her mother Gomti shouted at her, "Where were you? I have been calling you from such a long time." Gomti came closer to Aina, ready to slap her.

Aina begged, "Please don't beat me Ma." But Gomti wouldn't listen to her. She hit her hard again and again. It hurt terribly. "Ma, leave me."

And Aina actually screamed, "Leave me Ma. Don't beat me Ma. It hurts"."

Heera woke up again and patted Aina gently. He said, "Wake up Aina. You are seeing a nightmare again."

Deep in her nightmare, Aina looked confused. Heera wiped the beads of sweat from Aina's face and said, "In your dream, you saw Gomti, your mother who had brought you up. She used to beat you. But now your mother is Bijli. She is your real biological mother. She is very kind. She will never beat you."

Gradually, Aina's gasping breaths came back to normal and she clutched Heera desperately and said, "It was so real. I really felt that she was beating me cruelly. Heera don't leave me alone. Please stay with me always. Tell me that you will never leave me."

Heera said, "I will never leave you, I promise, my darling. Now just forget everything and just talk to me."

Heera became worried about Aina and he also started looking for jobs, but he had no experience from any reputed company, so he found it hard to get a job. His only experience had been with Daman Rai, the ex-husband of Aina, but Daman had not given him any certificate, so Heera found it hard to convince employers about his job experience.

Still Heera did not give up. He went on trying, but he realized that they would have to be careful with the money they had. Heera and Aina decided that they would live frugally and make the money last as much as they could. The constraints were now self imposed to save themselves from financial problems in the future, just in case they did not get any means of earning.

But Aina wanted to join College.

Aina said, "Heera, I want to study and I think that studies will make it easier to get a job. But if the fees is too much, then I can drop the idea."

"No Aina, it is a good idea that you should study. Education always comes in handy. We can afford your fees, so you should get admission in College."

"Should I opt for a co-ed college or should I go to a woman's college?"

"I think it is better to go to a woman's college."

"So you don't trust me."

"I don't trust boys. I know what dirty minds many of them have. They desire women and have a roving eye. You are too beautiful to be safe with boys."

"You Male Chauvinist Pig! Oh dear! How we women have to subjugate ourselves to our menfolk. Poor me! I have to bear the atrocities of my husband."

"Just you wait. I will show you what atrocities I can inflict on you."

"Heera, even if you tried, you couldn't hurt me. You love me too much for that. I think I can get away with murder with you. Thank you for loving me so much and being there for me always."

"I am there for you always, but see how contrary women are. Just now you were calling me an MCP and now you are telling me that I love you too much to hurt you. I don't think that any man has ever understood women, so why should I even try to understand you."

"But you know me very well and you understand me. I know that."

Heera said seriously, "Yes, I do Aina and that is why I respect and love you so much. You have a pure soul. Now coming to our problem, if you have to go to College, how can we manage Khushi?"

"Yes Heera, we cannot leave her alone with a servant and you cannot stay at home all the time I am away. This is a problem."

"The only way is that you call your mother and brother. I was telling them not to go away to Najapur, but they wouldn't listen, because they wanted us to have our privacy. Moreover I think that they did not want to be a financial burden on us. But now it is different. We need them. Write a letter telling them that they should not think about anything, but just come and live with us."

"You are strange. Most of the husbands want the mother-in-law to stay away, and here you are thinking of calling my mother to live permanently with us. But you are right. We will call Ma and Laila."

Aina wrote to her mother Bijli to come with Laila and stay with them permanently.

She wrote, "Ma, we need you. We are not calling you because you need our support. Heera and I are calling you because we need your support. I want to study and I need your help in looking after Khushi. See how selfish I have become. Laila must come too because I want him to be educated also. Please come as soon as you can, because my College starts next month. How is father? I hope he comes to stay with you."

CHAPTER 9

She dreamt again that night. "Aina was very happy because her grandfather Mahavir baba had come. Aina heard her brother Munna telling her, "Aina there are two balls kept in Baba's room. Come let us play with them." Aina ran to the outer room where Baba stayed. Baba was not there. Munna showed Aina the two special balls. They then sat on either side of the bed of Baba and started rolling the balls but once the two balls hit each other and they broke. A lot of smelly yellow and white stuff came out of them and dismayed, Aina and Munna looked at each other, because Baba's pristine white bed was dirty now with the mess. Just then Baba's personal servant Lalloo came up. He shouted, "You stupid children, these are not balls. These are eggs. Now you will be beaten up."

Aina and Munna ran away from Baba's room, afraid that they might be punished. Both tripped against each other and fell down and Munna started crying. Gomti came and slapped Aina at once, saying, "You are such a pest Aina. You always trouble Munna."

Then Gomti went away with her favourite son Munna, leaving Aina holding her stinging cheek with the red weal of the slap on it. And suddenly Aina started trembling as she felt that someone was stalking her.

She shouted, "Ma don't leave me."

But her mother went away. Aina felt lonely. She felt panic. She felt a sinking feeling and terror in her heart that welled up to consume her. The pain was unbearable. Tears slid helplessly down her cheeks and she felt afraid. She just felt more bereft and forsaken. She burst into tears again. She felt that no one loved her. She shouted, "Don't leave me alone"."

Then she heard the voice of someone. A soothing voice saying, "Aina, I am with you. I will never leave you." She felt strong arms holding her tight.

"Ah! My Heera! He will never leave me." And Aina nestled in those strong, caring arms and went to sleep again. In the morning she got up with a feeling of fear. She tried to control herself. She sat down and thought, "I have to be strong and brave. I should not pass on my fears to Khushi."

Aina started concentrating on Khushi. She wanted her to be physically healthy and mentally strong. She started taking Khushi to the courtyard behind, so that she could move about in the open. But one night Khushi developed high fever. Half the night she kept crying and both of them took turns cradling her and trying to get her to be quiet. But then they had to call the doctor. He told them that the fever must be because Khushi was teething. It was only when they gave medicines to Khushi, that she went to sleep and both of them slept for the remaining part of the night.

Aina started dreaming. "Heera and she were walking down the road with Khushi. Suddenly a man came. He had a pigeon's face. He suddenly grew long moustaches and his face suddenly changed and he became Rocoo. And all of a sudden Rocoo was coming to attack them and Aina took his gun and shot Rocoo. But Rocoo pulled at Khushi. "Leave her. Heera save Khushi. Save Khushi"."

Heera spoke up, "Aina, wake up, my darling. This is a nightmare that you are seeing. Now get up."

Aina opened her eyes and remembered a bit of her dream. She asked, "Heera, why do you think my nightmares have returned?"

"It may be because you are feeling scared of Rocoo again. Till now you thought that once he was in prison, we were safe, but now you may be feeling that he is capable of breaking prison and troubling us. On the face of it you don't realize it, but in your subconscious mind the fear must have opened up. Those fears may be triggering off your past memories, specially your traumatic childhood."

"Why am I so scared of everything?"

Heera came to Aina and said, "Because of your terrifying experiences. You are not to blame. Anyone who has suffered like you, would be a nervous wreck, but you are controlling your fears. Those who are fearless, have less problems. Those who have fears, show more courage when they curb their fears. Life is more difficult for them. You have fears but you are facing them and controlling yourself, so you are very brave."

CHAPTER 10

Next day she received a letter from Bijli, her mother, in which she had written that she would reach Kanpur within a fortnight.

Bijli wrote, "Laila and I have been missing you and Heera. Your father Kalka, stays mostly with his wife Gomti, because she is not keeping well, but he comes to meet me as much as he can. But Aina there has been such a change in the thinking of the society.

Till now it was considered that men could have a prostitute or a maharajin (cook) as their 'keep'. In a way, it exalted their position and status. But now it has become immoral and bad to 'keep' a woman. So to prevent censure, Kalka does not come to me as much as he used to. But health wise, he is better.

Laila and I are really looking forward to meeting Heera, Khushi and you. I will let you know the train timings. My love and blessings to you all. Ma"

Aina planned that her mother Bijli would stay in the second room. She prepared Khushi's room for her brother Laila. As soon as they arrived, Aina ran and hugged her mother and they started crying.

Laila stood quietly for some time, and then he said, "Heera. See how painful it is for the mother and daughter to think that they have to live together always permanently. That is why they both are crying."

Heera smiled and said, "You are right, Laila. But I think it is also a genetic disorder that Aina has inherited from her mother. They can't help crying."

"Just you wait, you naughty children. My hand may be small, but it hits hard," replied Bijli.

Both Heera and Laila started laughing.

Laila said, "Ma, you have such dainty hands. If you hit us, your hands will get hurt, but they will make no difference to our topography."

And that was the happy chord from that moment that tied them all together in a bond of affection, unity and harmony. Then Bijli said, "See, you want me to live here permanently, but there is one condition. You must take money from me, otherwise I will not stay here."

Heera resisted, "That is not right, Ma. We will not take anything from you. How can you think of such a thing? Children don't take money from their mothers. I know that you consider me less a son-in-law and more your son, so you shouldn't think about giving us money."

"But Heera, I don't want to be a burden on you."

"Elders give blessings. They are never a burden. You can never be a burden on us. It is our duty to look after our elders. Aina has lost her grandparents. Her father doesn't come here. I have no elders, no relatives. So for Aina and me, you are the only elder person who can be with us and we really want to look after you. I lost my mother very early, so I always yearned for the love of a mother. You have filled that vacuum, and I cannot take money from my mother," said Heera.

Bijli was touched and her eyes filled with tears as she said, "That is very sweet of you, Heera. All right, let us come to a compromise. If I sit idle, I will get senile sooner. So let me do something and whatever money comes from that, will be for the house expense. You have to agree to that or I will go back. I haven't opened my trunk yet, so it will be easy for me to return to Najapur. Now tell me if you accept this or not."

"Accepted. What do you plan to do?" asked Heera.

"I have knowledge of two things. Cooking and singing. I think that I can take singing and cooking classes. Ofcourse it will take time for me to get students, but I want to be busy."

"Ma, you will be busy. When I go to College, you will have to look after Khushi. That is a full time job."

"Aina, playing with my granddaughter is not a job, it is sheer pleasure. Okay, when you return from College then in the afternoon I can take the classes in my room. But how will I get students?"

Heera said, "I will put up posters to advertise your classes."

Bijli said, "Aina, you must also tell me what I should charge for the classes."

Aina said, "I will take an idea from other music teachers and then we can decide."

With the coming of Bijli and Laila, life became more of a celebration with the marvellous dishes that Bijli cooked and the laughter that revolved around Laila wherever he went. He certainly knew how to make everyone laugh.

Aina loved it when Bijli would sing her devotional songs and chant her mantras, early in the morning, while worshipping God. But Aina felt uneasy about herself and she asked Bijli, "Ma, do you think I am bad, because I don't feel like following rituals and rites."

"That doesn't matter Aina. You have a clear conscience and a clean heart. That is what really counts. I have yet to see you deliberately doing something wrong. You also never hurt other people knowingly. This is the best. What is the use of following rituals but being immoral? You are truthful and honest. The best is to be ethically good always and that you already are. So don't feel guilty at all."

Her mother was always able to make Aina feel good about herself and her life. The coming of her mother and brother also gave Aina more security and slowly the nightmares subsided. Till now Aina had never stayed with her biological mother Bijli for very long. Now they bonded well. Aina found a friend in Bijli and soon she was able to talk just about anything with her.

One day Aina asked, "Ma, is there any desire that you could never fulfil?"

"I belonged to a good family but my parents died in an accident. My father's brother was very poor. He sold me and those cruel people forced me to be a dancing girl. But then I met your father Kalka, and after that I belonged just to him. My one desire was that I should get married to him, but this wish can never be fulfilled, so why think about it."

"Ma, you never know what life has in store."

Aina felt the pain in her mother's heart and she gave her a tight hug. This bonding increased her sense of belonging and security, which she had never had when she had been with her father Kalka, who used to drink a lot, and his wife Gomti, who had brought Aina up.

Heera was also instrumental in lessening the nightmares, because he made it a point to make Aina feel secure. He gave her time and attention and he also tried to distract her from thinking a lot. So he took the whole family to see the city.

One day the tonga driver Rajan came to meet his brother Naren. He dropped in to see Heera who asked him if there was anything to see in Kanpur. When Rajan replied in the affirmative, Heera decided to tour the city. For the next few days, they went to see different places of the city. They spent the day having a picnic in Phool Bagh. Rajan took them through the main road of the city, The Mall Road, nearby.

He pointed to one room which was the last of a row of a barrack-like building and said, "It is said that here, freedom fighter Bhagat Singh asked to be inducted into the revolutionary party. When they refused to accept him, then he kept his hand over a candle flame without flinching, till the leaders accepted him."

Aina was distressed to see that no one was bothered about the historical significance of such a place and that the people around did not even seem to know its importance. Some of the parts of Kanpur were clean and beautiful, specially the Cantonment area, but many parts of the city were dirty and congested, but they enjoyed exploring the city. They went to see the Moti Jheel which was a lake near which, people would come and stroll in the evenings. They also went to see JK temple and the temple in Panki.

They went to see Massacre Ghat which was on the bank of the River Ganga. They also saw the Memorial gardens. Both these places had a significance during the First War of Indian Independence of 1857 against the British, when Kanpur was called Cawnpore.

They also went to Bithoor where it was said that there is a 'nail' marking the place where the God, Lord

Brahma, created the world. The historical significance of Bithoor was, that Rani Laxmi Bai of Jhansi had stayed there with the Peshwa and Nana Rao in her childhood. Laxmi Bai and Nana Rao had grown up to fight the British, in the First War of Independence in 1857.

CHAPTER 11

Heera took them to the Green Park stadium which was named after a British Lady Green who used to practice horse riding there. Behind was the River Ganga and on the other side was a College with its hostel. Heera bought tickets for the cricket match and all of them went there for all of the five days the Test match was played. It was like a picnic.

They carried thin mattresses and spread them out on the cemented stadium seats. Bijli and Aina would make lunch in the morning and they carried their tiffin carrier to the stadium. Bijli, Laila, Heera, Khushi and Aina reached the stadium before time, so that they could get good seats. And they enjoyed the match.

Whenever the Indian team did something good, the spectators would start dancing. It was highly entertaining, and they enjoyed themselves.

But on the fourth day, the people were more, but the tickets were less, as it was a Sunday. All of a sudden a huge crowd of students climbed the wall and entered the stadium. They tried to get into the stands and then the police had to take action. They started beating the students and the students resorted to pelting stones. After some time the situation was controlled by the police and after that the police personnel kept a watch over the stands, specially the stands for the students.

The game had been stopped for some time while the students were on the rampage. When things were under control, the game resumed. Aina then got so involved with the match that she literally jumped when suddenly she was tapped on the shoulder by a rod.

She realized that a policeman was standing near her. She looked up and to her amazement, she saw Inspector Verma standing in the aisle near her. He looked at Aina and said, "You were the lady connected with the Rocoo case and burning of Maakhan, right?"

Aina just nodded her head. Heera too saw Verma at the same time and he greeted, "How are you, Inspector? Are you stationed here in Kanpur?"

"Yes, but where did you disappear all of a sudden? I went to your house after Rocoo had been caught, but it was locked. Why didn't you tell me that you were going away?"

Heera was honest with him and he said, "We decided to leave Rojpur because it wasn't safe for us there. When we decided to leave, we thought of telling you. But Rocoo had hinted to us that he had a man in your police station, so I didn't tell you, because I didn't want anyone to know that we were leaving Rojpur. I am sorry about that, but it was just for Aina's and our daughter Khushi's safety. Where is Rocoo now?"

"He is in Lucknow jail serving his sentence, so you need not be afraid of him anymore."

"That is a comforting thing to know. I hope he doesn't escape again."

"No chance of that. By the way, Daman Rai had contacted me to find out about Maakhan. I did not tell him that Maakhan was in hospital."

Heera asked, "Was Maakhan put in jail?"

"No. I could not make a case against Maakhan. Actually I had wanted your wife to testify against him, but you both were not available, so I had to let him go."

"Did Maakhan go back to Daman?" asked Aina.

"I was transferred to Kanpur, so I don't know what happened to Rocoo or Maakhan."

"So is Maakhan still free?" asked Aina.

"As far as I know, yes. Okay. Bye. You can come to me if you have any work."

Inspector Verma walked away and Heera muttered, "God forbid that we have any work ever where we would need the police."

At the end of the day's play, they went home. They were tired, but happy. As they retired for the night, Aina said, "What a co-incidence that we should meet Inspector Verma today."

"It was good that we met him. Aina, now you can be at peace because Rocoo is in prison."

"Are you sure he will not escape again?"

"Inspector Verma was quite sure and we will take his word for it"

"What if Maakhan is sent after us?"

"He will not be able to find us amidst the crowd in Kanpur."

"But Inspector Verma found us, even though it was just accidental."

"No one will trouble us anymore. Stop thinking about the past. Now your ordeal is over Aina. You are finally free from your ex husband Daman, from Rocoo, and most of all from your emotional demons. Don't be afraid any more. You had seemed to be afraid of everything when I first met you."

"Yes I was afraid of death and of life, of people and of ghosts, of making a mistake, and so many, many other things," said Aina.

"But now you build up your inner wall of steel more and then you will never suffer from fears again."

"So you knew what I was going through?! You understand me so well," said Aina.

"I know what you are thinking, before you know it," smiled Heera. He bent over her and his lips touched her cheeks and her eyelids. He then wiped her tears with his lips. He kissed her with small caresses all over her soft face. She thrilled to him and caught him.

"Don't you hate me for being such a weak and scared person?"

Heera said, "On the contrary, I admire you. You are such a lovely person. I want to make you very happy. I often dream how we will be together the next time. I think that I will kiss you here and here and here."

He kissed her on the nape of her neck. She pressed herself against him. He gathered her in his arms and made her lie down, while he knelt on the floor. He slowly caressed her head, gently without threatening her with too much ardour.

She had shut her eyes and he said, "You have suffered, my precious darling. I will see to it that now you keep smiling and laughing always. My love will be a balm to you. If anyone comes to hurt you, I will be there to stop the hurt. I will protect you, my love."

He could not control himself anymore and he realized that she didn't want him to control himself. He slowly touched her and she shivered. She became aware of her body as never before. She had never realized that making love could be so pleasing.

She felt a rush of blood. She then felt the soft breeze of the heavens. She felt Nature at its best whispering love to her soul. She felt the breeze rage into a storm. And then they shared together exquisite peace. Satisfying and fulfilling.

They still held each other. It seemed as if Heera could not leave her, as he started again. She thought she could not take it anymore, but soon both of them felt the ecstasy again.

"I never knew it could be like this."

"You will get such love from me always. Now you will have this happiness forever," said Heera.

"I believe you Heera, and I cherish your totally unconditional love too. It has made me free of all my complexes. I don't need to think now whether I am doing the right thing or not. I know that I can rely on my instincts because they are usually right, but even if they are wrong, so what? I am ready to face the resulting repercussions. My motto is made. It is simple. I should give love and not take hate from anyone. I don't have the urge to take revenge anymore. I have forgotten the past and forgiven others and myself for everything."

Heera caressed her hair, saying, "I understand."

"And that is why I love you so much Heera. You make me feel special. You give me time and attention. You console me when I am hurt. You do not think that when I am serious and quiet, then I am sulking, but you understand that it is because I am feeling pain. You love me for what I am and not for what you want me to be. You have patience to accept my moods. This is what I wanted always. Thank you."

"I am glad I have given you what you wanted."

Aina said, "Today I am free in my mind. I am comfortable with who I am. I want to live and let others live in the way they want, except when they are immoral. Heera, tell me your philosophy of life."

"Milady, I am a simple man. I just think that we should face every event of life with honesty and courage. There need not be a hallowed pursuit of truth. There need not be a severance from normal living, but even in a routine life, we should be good, true and honest."

"But, Heera, what is truth according to you?"

"If we take ethical decisions throughout life, we would be pure and genuine and that is what truth is. Ethical decisions can be defined in the way that, we should not do anything we are ashamed of. We should not do anything that we would be embarrassed to tell our parents or our children."

How uncomplicated Heera was! Dear faithful Heera! How lucky she was to have him as a support. He just loved her for what she was, with nary a thought of anything else. He made her happy. She had to admit that it was extremely comforting to know that Heera was there for her, like a rock to lean on.

CHAPTER 12

Aina got admission for her graduation and she started going to College. She was relieved that Khushi did not cry too much on seeing her go everyday. Khushi did not trouble Bijli much either. When Aina returned from College one day and hugged Khushi, Bijli said, "Don't feel guilty about leaving Khushi everyday and don't worry about Khushi. We get on famously together. Khushi is a happy child. She adjusts very easily."

Aina answered, "I am happy that Khushi accepts my daily absence, but she is only two years old. I feel guilty that I leave her, but I know that you look after her well, so I don't worry about her."

The college opened up a new world for her. She met other girls and saw the way they dressed, they were more modern than the girls at Najapur or Rojpur. She asked Heera, "I have always worn a sari. Can I wear shalwar suits?"

Heera had no objections, but he said, "Don't get extremely tight ones made."

Aina replied, "Don't worry. I don't like extremely tight ones myself. I will never follow fashion blindly. I will always wear things that suit me and look decent on me."

"I know that, so Aina there is no need for you to ask me. You can do what you want."

"Thank you. But you ask me before doing anything, so I should also ask you. This has to be an equal partnership. The same rules apply to both of us."

The trend for tight suits had started because of film heroines. The figure-hugging top long kurtas were extremely tight till the knees, so much so that it was difficult for girls wearing them, to climb buses and cycle rickshaws. There were other fashion rages like puffed sleeves in sari blouses and the hair being cut in a fringe. Even young men wore extremely tight trousers.

Heera took Bijli and Aina to a Kavi Sammelan, (a poet's meet). In it, one poet, who excelled in the comic strain, regaled the audience by making fun of the tight clothes of girls and the tight drain-pipe trousers worn by the boys. The heroines had also inspired the trend for huge bouffonts as a hairstyle. One poet made fun of the huge buns that were the fashion, by reciting verses of glasses and cups being kept inside the buns of the girls to make them look huge. It was hilarious.

Later Aina got two sets of comfortable suits made for herself. It made her feel that she was more modern, but one day, she realized how conventional she still was in the eyes of the so-called modern people. On the way to her College, some boys called her 'Vintage.' Aina heard this, but then she heard another boy say, "She is the only girl here who is dressed decently and you all are mocking her by calling her 'Vintage'."

That made her feel good, but she had more to learn. Aina realized what modernity had really started to mean when the next day she was on the Mall Road on her way to her College. Everything appeared normal, when suddenly she felt that people were stopping in their tracks and looking behind her. Even scooter riders and motorcyclists stopped and looked behind her.

She also looked back and what she saw made her realize the cause for the sudden stoppage of all traffic. A car had stopped and three girls had got off from the car. They were all wearing very tight pants and Tshirts. They wore huge goggles and had bob cut hair. The sight was too much for the conventional regional city of Kanpur, which was used to seeing fully clad girls.

The traffic remained stalled and mouths remained open till the girls crossed the street, bought something from a shop and came back to their car. Only when they were seated and driven off, did the traffic resume its busy-ness. But remarks could still be heard from the pedestrians, "Oh! How shameless these girls are!" "Imagine being dressed like boys and wearing pants and tight fitting shirts that leave nothing to the imagination. I hope they don't spoil our daughters!"

Aina came home and related the incident to Bijli and Laila. Bijli was scandalized that girls could wear pants. She said, "What is this world coming to! How can girls wear clothes that show the full outline of their body."

Laila said, "Just see the irony. I feel comfortable in feminine wear, but I can't wear it, and here are girls who are wearing men's clothes."

Soon Aina became very popular in College which was only for girls. A thing that surprised her was the adulation she got from the other girls. A beautiful girl, Binny became her friend and Binny loved to sit in class holding Aina's hand, which made Aina very uncomfortable. Aina was totally unaware of her charm, so she could not understand the adoration she got.

There was a girl Manjula, who would stand afar and just look at Aina during the recess. One day, Binny told Aina that Manjula wanted to hear Aina sing. Aina refused, only to be taken aback when she saw Manjula start crying when Binny told her that Aina would not sing.

Aina also tried her hands at extra curricular activities like debates and different sports, and did considerably well in them. She started enjoying the freedom and light atmosphere of College life.

Moreover for the first time, Aina was very naughty. She had become quite a leader and she often troubled the teachers. The History subject was taught to them by the Principal in her office. Once the Principal walked out for five minutes to meet a parent, Aina polished off the sweets kept on a side table. When the Principal came back, she was mystified as to where the sweets had gone, but she had no evidence to blame it on the students. So Aina went scot free.

Once, the girls were getting very bored by her lecture, so the moment the Principal walked out, Aina climbed onto the side table, and advanced the time of the clock by half an hour. Then when the Principal came back, she looked at the clock, called the peon and told him to ring the bell, much to the amazement of the whole college. These antics needed a lot of courage, for actually, the old Principal was a very stern and austere disciplinarian, whom all the students were very afraid of.

At home too, the atmosphere became more relaxed. Aina slept well as she was no longer troubled by nightmares. Moreover Laila kept them entertained with his jokes, witty one-liners and his antics.

One day Heera came and said, "Ma, I have put posters at some shops and outside our gate."

Bijli thanked him and Laila said, "Putting posters is not enough to make tuition classes a success. People should hear that music classes are going on here. Ma, I am your first student. Take this as fees." And Laila gave her a rose that he had plucked from the courtyard.

Bijli said, "Laila, you know how to sing. You don't need classes."

"All the more reason to show the neighbours how well your students sing."

Laila forced Bijli to sit down and teach him and then he took out the strangest, the weirdest and the most tuneless sounds.

Aina said, "Laila, students will run away rather than come here if they hear you sing like this."

Laila told Bijli, "Ma, no one appreciates my talent. Just look at your daughter, Aina. She has not understood the depth of my music. There is music everywhere in Nature. Even animals and birds have music in their voices. So why can't I imitate the music in the voice of a donkey?"

Bijli replied seriously, "My child, don't bother. It takes wisdom to recognize talent and Aina has none."

"Well said, Ma," said Laila, and Aina, Bijli and Laila laughed. Laila said, "Why are you laughing, Aina? Ma called you a fool."

"Laila, I am laughing because I am a fool because I listen to you. But seriously Laila, you are a breath of fresh air in our house."

Yes, it was true that Laila made others laugh, but Laila was laughed at also. Urchins ran after him on the streets imitating his feminine walk and commenting on him. The shopkeepers would make fun of him if he went to purchase something. It was demeaning.

CHAPTER 13

One day Laila was returning home after the frustration of not getting a job anywhere. Suddenly an eunuch accosted Laila and said, "You are an eunuch, but I haven't seen you in the colony where we stay."

Laila replied, "I stay with my sister."

"But that is not allowed. You should come and stay in the eunuch colony. Are you new to Kanpur?" When Laila replied in the affirmative, the eunuch said, "I am Ratna. You should come with me and I will introduce you to our Sheela guru. Then you can stay with us."

Laila politely declined. Ratna started pestering Laila. Just then they realized that some young men had gathered around them. One young man said, "Why are you two wasting your time talking? Your job is to sing and dance. Now start singing and dancing for us."

Ratna replied, "Go away. Don't trouble us."

Another young man said, "But you have a duty to entertain everyone. Come on sing and dance."

Ratna picked up a stone and said, "Back off. Leave us alone or I will pelt you with stones."

The men did not back off. All of them started intoning like a chant, "Come on sing and dance."

Ratna looked furious and Laila softly said, "Ratna, it is better that we run away. There are too many people here. They will beat us hollow."

Laila turned around and started running away towards his house. Laila looked back to see that Ratna was right behind him. The crowd was still chasing them, but a flock of sheep had impeded their speed.

Meanwhile Aina had come back from her College and she was sitting in the verandah with her mother. Suddenly Laila caught Ratna's hand and ran into the verandah. Laila gasped, "This person is Ratna. Many people are after us."

Aina shouted, "Go inside and hide. Don't let them see you here."

Ratna hesitated and then he said, "Are you sure that I can enter your house?"

Laila shouted, "Yes, ofcourse," and he pulled Ratna into the house.

Aina and Bijli kept sitting in the verandah as if nothing had happened. They saw a group of about twenty people stop and look around, but after some time, they went away. Aina and Bijli then went inside and shut the front door. They found Ratna in tears. "Why were the men after you?" asked Aina.

Ratna spoke up with tears in his eyes, "They were ready to attack us just because we are eunuchs. What is our life! We are respected by nobody. We have a bad time. We have no support from any one. We are destitute. We are forsaken and estranged from our family and we are ostracized by society. We have a problem earning our livelihood. Moreover our female body and psyche, is trapped in a male body, and this suffocates and stifles us. On top of that, there is no one in this world we can call our own. Wherever we go people are ready to attack and hit us."

Laila said, "Ratna, you were telling me to go and live with you all, but see what you face. I am lucky that I have a family which is ready to keep me with them. So now don't pester me to go and stay with you all."

Aina had made tea for Ratna and Laila, and Ratna said tearfully, "Laila, I will not pester you because I have come to know that you are happy here. But let me warn you. Other eunuchs will pester you and our Sheela guru too would want you to stay with us."

Laila said, "Will they force me to stay there?"

Ratna said, "Yes. I will not tell them, but if they come to know that you stay here, they might."

Aina said, "I will go and talk to your Sheela guru if they pester Laila. I have started teaching Laila to study. I can also teach all of you, if you want. Ratna, you can come here to study."

Ratna answered, "What will I do with studies!"

"You can do a lot. You can study and then give your tenth examination."

Ratna replied, "I will see. Laila, you are really lucky to have such a loving family."

Ratna went away but after about a week, she came to their house and told Laila, "I didn't tell anyone, but Sheela guru has come to know about you staying here. She wants you to come and stay with us."

Laila asked, "Will she use force?"

Ratna said, "See, she is a typical guru. The woman in the guru makes her feel motherly toward us, but the man in her makes her aggressive and that results in her wanting her way always. See, generally eunuch gurus are very considerate, but you should keep it in mind that Sheela guru is like a dictator. She is such a strong person that nobody defies her."

"If I come to stay with you all, what will I have to do?" asked Laila.

Ratna said, "We perform at weddings, or when a child is born. We sing and dance to bless the newlyweds or the newborn and we get cash or in kind."

Laila said, "I have done all this before."

Aina had been sitting quietly, listening to them talking. She now asked, "What is the reason that you all have to sing and dance?"

Ratna explained, "We believe that when Lord Ram was going for exile, many people followed him into the forest. He told all the men and women to go back to Ayodhya. So the men and women went back, but the eunuchs, who were neither men nor women, kept waiting for Lord Ram till his return from exile. When Lord Ram returned after fourteen years, he found all those people still waiting for him at the same place."

Aina asked, "Did they stand for fourteen years?"

Ratna said, "Yes, that is what is said. Impressed by their devotion, Rama granted them the boon to bless people during auspicious occasions like childbirth and weddings. This started our custom of singing and dancing, and giving blessings."

Laila asked, "How can I save myself from this?"

Ratna asked, "Why don't you start dressing like a man? Then no one will be the wiser."

Laila said, "I don't think I would be comfortable. I feel like a woman in a man's body."

Ratna asked, "Go and live somewhere else."

Laila said, "Kanpur is so crowded, that it is not easy to find a rented house. We are lucky that we found this house. Moreover, till when can I keep running away from reality. Wherever I go, this problem will dog my footsteps. Isn't it better to come to terms with it?"

"Then I think you should come one day and convince Sheela guru that you are better off here."

Laila said, "But if I come to the colony, Sheela guru may hold me captive."

Ratna asked, "That is a strong possibility."

Laila said, "So I will not take a chance. Let her make the first move, then I will see."

CHAPTER 14

Aina and Bijli were still talking with Laila, when Heera came. He went inside to freshen up. Just as Aina got up to make tea for him, they heard Heera scream loudly. In a trice Laila, Aina and Bijli ran inside to see what had happened, but the door of the bedroom was bolted from inside. They banged at the door but there was no response.

Bijli shouted, "Break the door. Something drastic must have happened." But the door was too sturdy to break. Thankfully the door had small glass panes and one pane was broken. Laila put his hand in and opened the latch. They rushed inside.

Her heart beating with fear, Aina reached first and then she asked, "What happened, Heera? Why are you standing on the stool?"

Heera gasped, "I am scared of those creatures."

Afraid that some ferocious animal had found its way inside, Aina turned around. Heera was pointing at something on the floor and Aina followed the direction his finger pointed to, and then she burst out laughing.

Laila and Bijli seemed quite perplexed that Aina was laughing hysterically, while Heera looked petrified. Through her laughter, Aina told them, "Heera is afraid of that tiny cockroach." They looked down and saw that, oblivious of the panic it had created in Heera, a small cockroach had stopped to rest on the floor.

Laila and Bijli also burst out laughing, while Heera looked decidedly sheepish. But Heera just refused to step down from the high stool. It was only when Laila had swept away the cockroach that Heera climbed down from the stool, saying, "I can face any other animal but, I am terrified of cockroaches. Don't take Khushi that side. It may climb on Khushi."

Aina said, "Heera, I know you are frightened and it is not easy to control fears, but speak in a calm voice otherwise you will pass on this fear of cockroaches to Khushi. However afraid we might be, we need to talk in a normal voice, so that Khushi is not scared."

That night Heera said, "I feel so foolish that I am afraid of cockroaches. How do we develop these fears?"

Aina replied, "I am learning in psychology that the time of birth upto five years, is the time when the child is most susceptible. Some nasty experience can cause the fear, or elders can transfer their fears to them."

"Do you think I had a nasty experience with a cockroach in my childhood?"

"Could be. Heera, I am full of fears too, so you don't have to be defensive about your fears, but just do not pass on the fears to Khushi. Because I fear so many things, it is my desire that my children should be totally fearless and brave."

Heera said, "I have another thing to discuss with you. I was reading in the papers about family planning. We should do something about it."

"But isn't it wrong to impede Nature?"

"No. The population is increasing so alarmingly that the promotion of family planning in India has been proposed. You don't have to do anything. There is no surgery involved, no termination of the birth of a child.

The government has started the commercial sale of Nirodh which is a condom that men have to use. It will help us to space out the birth of our next child."

"How shameless of you to talk about it!"

"There is no shame. Today I will buy Nirodh."

But it was very difficult. Aina stood far away from the shop and Heera went to purchase Nirodh, and suddenly he felt tongue tied. Whenever he tried to ask for it, some other customer would come and Heera would clam up. He stood there for fifteen minutes and Aina started fretting at the delay. Finally the shopkeeper too lost his patience. He asked with irritation, "What is it that you want?" And then all Heera could do was point at the advertisement of Nirodh.

The shopkeeper suddenly grinned and picked up the packets. Heera wished to do it unobtrusively, but the shopkeeper just kept them on the counter and Heera became red with embarassment. When Heera explained by actions, then the shopkeeper gave him a carry bag. Heera gave the money quickly and rushed away from the shop. This happened on three visits to the same shop. After that it was a cakewalk for Heera as the shopkeeper had started recognizing Heera and he would quietly and quickly give him the packets in a carry bag.

But it was already too late for family planning because Aina had already become pregnant.

Everyday Aina would go to College on a bicycle till one day Bijli said, "Why don't you arrange a rickshaw for Aina. In these days, Aina should not ride a bicycle."

"What days?" asked Laila.

"Why can't Aina ride a bicycle?" asked Heera.

Bijli said, "Because you two nutcases, she is going to have a baby."

Laila and Heera let out loud cries of sheer happiness which made Aina run out of her room. She saw Laila and Heera dancing with aplomb. Soon Bijli and Aina were forced to join in. From that day they took extra care of Aina. And Heera took a telephone landline so that it would be easy to communicate with Aina at home.

CHAPTER 15

One day Laila was going to look for a job, when three eunuchs came and stood in front of him. The one who was the tallest, said, "I am Najma. Sheela guru has sent us. He wants that you should live with us. He says that it is better that we stay together and maintain our unity. You have to come as no one refuses her order."

Laila said, "Would you refuse to stay with your family if they gave you love and respect? Be a friend to me and tell me how I can continue to stay with my family. I will do what you three say."

Najma replied, "Meet Sheela guru. He will get miffed if you flout his orders. He is like a dictator, but he is very fair and just. See if you can convince him."

"Come on, I will meet him," said Laila.

They took Laila through narrow lanes to a colony where everyone was an eunuch. Laila was quite nervous because if Sheela guru got angry, he might command the others to harm him. But he calmly walked towards Sheela guru who turned to look at him and then both convulsed into laughter.

"Sheela. Imagine you are Sheela guru. I never imagined to find you here. You were working for the Nawab of Najapur, how did you come here?"

"Welcome Laila. This is a pleasant surprise. The Nawab died and his son did not want me to work for him, so I came to Kanpur. Here I started living in this colony and now I am the guru here."

Laila said, "Sheela, I have found my sister and I am living with her. Please allow me to stay with her. She has a daughter who is my life. I know that I should stay here with you all, but I can't live without my family."

"Laila, all the eunuchs will feel cheated because I have forced them to stay here, but all right, you can stay with your family. I cannot forget the day when you saved me from the police who had thought that I had stolen the Nawab's necklace. Really, it was so nice of you that you had said that I had been with you at the feast, so I could not have stolen the necklace."

"It was a white lie and it harmed no one, but it saved you. I knew you could not steal. It was not your fault and you had just been a bit drunk and had been in your room, but the police would not have believed you."

"But I will be eternally grateful to you. You can go and stay with your family."

"But what about the other eunuchs?"

"I will order them not to trouble you. No one will have the courage to go against me."

Laila felt very happy and he thanked Sheela guru and came back home and told the family.

Bijli commented, "A good deed always comes back where it starts. You helped Sheela guru in the past and that good deed has saved you today."

Aina also was very comforted when Laila told him that Sheela guru was his friend, but the fear still gnawed at her that the other eunuchs might take out their anger on Laila.

Now Laila had to take a few decisions. "How can I make something out of my life?"

Laila felt that education would be a way out for him. He also decided that he would not embarrass his family any more by wearing feminine clothes, though they had never said anything to him. He bought two trousers and two shirts for himself and then he started dressing up in men's clothes.

Though on seeing his mannerisms and hearing his voice, people could realize that he was an eunuch, but atleast it was not as much obvious, as it had been when he wore feminine clothes, specially as he was a good looker with his fair skin and big eyes.

Laila had a burning ambition to do something worthwhile. He wanted to obliterate the handicap of his sexuality by proving himself in some field. It was not easy for him. He couldn't do a job or start any business because people would not accept him. He started looking for avenues to achieve something, so that he could raise his esteem in his own eyes.

One thing that fascinated him was politics. He loved to read the newspaper. Aina had taught him enough to read and write, and then he would discuss politics with Heera and Aina.

Aina told him one day, "You have a flair and understanding of politics and you are good with words. You should be in politics as you are a very good orator."

Laila answered, "No one will vote for me. Who will accept an eunuch in politics?"

Bijli said, "Laila, a time will come when eunuchs will be accepted in politics and respected by society. It is just a matter of time. You mark my words that in your lifetime, you will be given respect by these very people who have humiliated you. Just have patience."

Laila replied, "Ma, what a great thing you have said! What you have said means a lot to me. Thank you so much. You are a lovely mother to have. I am so lucky that you consider me your child."

Bijli said, "Laila, my blessings are with you."

Laila said, "I don't think that I will get a job anywhere. I think that the only way is to go back to singing and dancing like before. I can stay here and go with Sheela guru's eunuchs, then come back here."

"Laila, you told me that you want to achieve something as you do not enjoy singing and dancing. Study and get educated and then you will become a force to reckon with. Maybe society is not accepting you, but books will not reject you. Even if you are not accepted in a job, you can write for magazines and newspapers, put your point across and help others."

Aina finally convinced Laila and he came to a decision and he said, "Aina, you are right. I should get educated, instead of going through this frustration. Can you give more time to teach me?"

"Ofcourse, Laila." Aina and Laila started taking Laila's studies very seriously.

But Laila had a naughtiness about him too which he often used on people with comic results. A bachelor Sanad lived in a room near their house. Sanad was of medium height and thin, but his face had sharp features. He seemed a shy and reserved person who would not talk much. Still he was polite towards Heera, Aina and Bijli, but he ignored Laila in the beginning.

Laila would greet Sanad but would get no answer. Laila remained quiet for two days because it hurt him that a neighbor was not accepting him. But Laila was not a person who could stop himself for long. After two days when Sanad did not give an answer to his greeting, Laila went and accosted him directly. Sanad would not look at him. Then Laila said deliberately, "What if you were born an eunuch and I had refused to look at you as a human being. What would you have done? It is not my fault that I am an eunuch. Nature made me like this. I am suffering the curse of it already. Why are you increasing my suffering by ignoring me?"

And Sanad started talking to Laila. They never became good friends, but Sanad enjoyed conversations with Laila, as Laila was full of laughter and fun, even though Laila made a fool of Sanad on many occasions. Sanad was gullible and would easily believe whatever Laila told him, though much of this belief was because Laila had a great convincing power.

One movie was making a lot of news because of the fear factor. Laila had seen the movie. He came back and told Sanad, "The film is so scary that pregnant ladies are not allowed inside because of the fear, that out of fear, they may deliver their children in the auditorium. The theatre people have put a lady doctor on the job to check the women before they enter."

Sanad went and saw the movie and came back and said, "Laila. I checked all the entrances and exits of the movie hall, but I saw no lady doctor anywhere."

Sanad was surprised why everyone laughed.

After some days, Sanad came shyly to invite their family for his wedding, but they could not go to attend because the wedding was in Lucknow. They decided to make up for it by decorating the house of Sanad before his new bride entered his house.

Aina welcomed them and she even cooked a lavish dinner for the two. The bride Usha was quite sweet, though quite plain looking, but she was shy as behoved a new bride. Everything went off well, but Sanad seemed very worried about something. Aina kept on asking him what the matter was, but Sanad did not tell her or Heera anything. Sanad had finished his dinner, so Aina told Sanad to take his bride and go home, but Sanad just kept sitting.

It became so embarrassing when Sanad would not get up, that Aina escorted Usha to her new home. Khushi had gone to sleep, so Heera went inside to settle her on her bed. Left alone with Laila, Sanad quickly said, "Laila, I am in a fix. I don't know what to do on the first night. I thought my elder brother would tell me, but he didn't and I was too shy to ask him. Can you tell me?"

"Ofcourse, Sanad. Now listen carefully. First you should go and touch the feet of your bride six times even if she tells you not to. Then you have to make her sit and worship her there. You must then blow a conch shell thrice. The rest your bride will do."

"Are you sure this has to be done?"

Laila said, "Ofcourse, Sanad. I never tell lies. All the best, Sanad. Have a happy first night."

When Sanad reached his house, Aina came away, leaving Sanad with his bride Usha. Then Laila told Heera and Aina about the joke he had played on Sanad. They had a hearty laugh.

Aina said, "I don't think that he will follow your instructions." Soon they all got busy washing the used crockery. A few minutes later, Aina nearly dropped a plate when she heard the sound of the conch shell being blown, and then all of them were rolling with laughter.

Aina wiped the tears of laughter streaming down her face and said, "Laila, you are really incorrigible. The poor bride will be thinking she has married a mad man or a hermit. Laila, you are the limit."

"Aina, what about Sanad? Wasn't it the limit of irony and the height of insensitivity that he asked an eunuch about what to do on his first wedding night?"

Aina froze and she quickly looked away, because she had seen the raw hurt in the eyes of Laila. She realized that Laila always laughed and made others laugh, but beneath it was a deep sadness that Laila did not let others see. Her heart was filled with compassion for the way Laila suffered, and admiration for the way that Laila hid his pain from even his near and dear ones.

CHAPTER 16

Bijli first got two students to learn music from her. She took fifty rupees a month from each child as tuition fee. The family celebrated that day by going to see a movie. After that Bijli made a lovely dinner which everyone enjoyed. Soon life fell into a groove.

Aina would go to College in the morning and return by afternoon. They would have lunch and then, Bijli would take her music classes. Gradually her students increased to ten. The worrying fact was that neither Heera nor Laila were getting any job. Aina started worrying about their financial condition.

One day Aina asked Heera, "You manage all the finances and tell me not to worry, but let me know our financial position."

"Your alimony of two lakhs that we had got, is still intact and I have kept it in the bank so that we can earn interest on it. But slowly my saving of one lakh is getting spent as we have no income except for the tuition fees that Ma gets. Things are worrisome because we don't want to spend the alimony money. Now the value of money is also going down and Laila and I are not getting jobs."

Bijli had walked in just then and she had heard Heera. She said, "You don't worry Heera. This is the result of the cost of living going up. In my childhood, we could buy the provisions for our houschold in just ten rupees, but now it costs three times more. What is this world coming to! Heera. Take this money, This is the fees that the children have given me for their classes."

Heera said, "Ma, do you realize that you are the only one out of us who is earning. The rest of us are sponging on you. I am just not able to get a job, even though I am ready to do any work. The only condition is that the work should not compromise my honesty."

Bijli replied, "I wish I could do more for you all. I am the oldest. I should be managing the complete expenses of the household. I have some savings if you ever need them, Heera."

"I will ask you if we need to, but let us hope that we don't need to ever ask you for your savings. I am also thinking of investing a part of my savings."

One day Aina returned from College to see a man sitting in the verandah talking to her mother. Just then Laila also came and Bijli said, "I am sorry, but I didn't understand a word of what you have been saying. Explain it to my children."

The man said, "I am an LIC agent."

"What is that?"

"It is for insurance of your life. Just think if you die . . ."

Laila felt offended and retaliated immediately, "Why should I think that I will die? Let my enemies die. I want to live. I don't want to hear your rubbish."

"Let me complete Sir. I am from the Life Insurance Corporation of India which has been created with the objective of spreading life insurance to provide adequate financial cover at a reasonable cost. It is not only on the contingency of death, but it can also be taken as an investment and save money. There are many policies that are good for your future."

Laila replied, "Why talk of the future when I don't have a job now? Can you get me a job?"

Heera came in just then and finally he was receptive to what the harried Insurance agent had to say. Heera took a policy and the agent was satisfied.

Even Aina had started thinking that she should start earning. So she got Laila to put up some posters for tuitions for junior classes. She got one student whom she taught when Khushi slept in the afternoon. Gradually her students also increased to five. She also started pooling to the household kitty.

That afternoon when Aina came home, she saw that her mother was talking to Usha in the courtyard. When she went to her room, she heard Laila speaking in his room, "Now listen to this one. It is called a limerick.

'I once sat next to a Duchess at tea
Distressed as a person could be
Her rumblings abdominal
Were simply phenomenal
And everybody thought it was me.'

Did you like it? Yes, you smiled. Beautiful!"

Aina was curious to know who the visitor was to whom Laila was telling the limerick. She walked to Laila's room and looked inside. Then she said, "Laila, there is no one except Khushi here. To whom are you telling this limerick?"

"I am telling it to Khushi. You will see that she will grow up to be a very humorous person like me."

"And I would love that, because wherever you go, you make everyone happy. I am so proud of you."

"Thank you Aina. By the way, if any eunuchs come here, you don't come out. Today Najma accosted me. She said that it was not fair that I was permitted to stay away from the colony. In a way she threatened me."

"I hope they will not hurt you?"

"I sincerely hope not," said Laila seriously.

A few days later Aina was very worried. Laila had said that he would come back in one hour, but he hadn't returned. He had not come back for lunch even. It was nearly four hours since he had gone. Aina had no way to tell Heera about this, as Heera had gone to explore the prospect of a job which had been advertised in the newspaper. Ma was taking her music classes and Khushi was sleeping, so Aina paced the courtyard.

Just then Sanad came and greeted Aina. She asked him, "Have you seen Laila anywhere?"

"Yes, he is with many workers in front of the factory in the next lane."

"What is he doing there?"

"He was giving a speech to all the workers who are on strike and I must say that he speaks very well. I stopped and listened to him. He should become an orator."

Sanad went into his house and Aina relaxed, content that Laila was all right, but just then she saw Laila running towards her. She stood up in consternation and saw him coming into the courtyard. He then stopped and she saw that Laila was totally out of breath.

Before she could say anything, he said, "Don't worry. Everything is all right. I was with the workers. I am sorry I am late. You must be worried, but I couldn't help it. I am just coming."

Laila rushed in and Aina made a cup of tea for him. When he came, Aina gave him a packet of biscuits and he was so hungry that he ate up all the biscuits in the packet, even as he told her what had happened.

It seemed that he had been walking past the factory gate, when he saw five workers shouting slogans as they walked out of the factory. One worker Naren was known to him because he lived in their colony and was the brother of the tonga driver Rajan.

When he asked Naren what had happened, Naren told him that one manager had become angry that the stipulated amount of goods had not been made. He would not listen to Naren when he told him that the reason for the less production was, that a machine had been out of order. The Manager had slapped Naren, though it was not his fault. Then all the five workers who had been working on that machine, had supported Naren and they had staged a walk-out. But the other workers in the factory had not come to know about this.

Laila said, "I felt bad for Naren, so I told him to fight for his rights. Naren stammers, therefore he could not speak for himself. So I started explaining what had happened and Aina, I don't know how it happened, but the crowd started getting larger. Finally all the workers decided to support Naren. Now all of them are on strike."

"And you have become a union leader."

"Aina, I had to speak for Naren."

"Ofcourse, but why were you running?"

"Don't ask me, please Aina."

"Did you meet anyone from the eunuch colony? Did they threaten you? Did the police beat the workers? Did they beat you? Are you hurt? Tell me at once."

"How negative you are Aina. You are thinking of bad things only. Don't insist please."

"Laila, you have to tell me."

"I had to go to the toilet and I couldn't wait."

Aina laughed and said, "You stopped your speech and ran, just to go to the toilet."

Laila said, "Well, what else could I have done?"

Just then Naren came and stammered, "The Mmm . . . a . . . nnn . . . age . . . mmment has suspended that mmm . . . a . . . nnn . . . ager. We have . . . wwo . . . nn our case and it is because of you, Laila. Thank you so mmmm . . . uch."

Laila shouted with joy, "I have done it finally. I am worth something." Aina hugged him.

Laila had finally found his vocation.

CHAPTER 17

One evening Usha and Sanad came to meet them. Laila, Bijli, Heera and Aina welcomed them over tea and snacks, and they talked.

Usha said, "Do you know that a new stove has come in the market. It will be given with a gas cylinder in which there will be LPG which is a fuel. A salesman had come yesterday to sell one to me but I felt so afraid. What if the cylinder bursts? It must be so risky."

Bijli replied, "But I have heard that it is a very good thing. Now if a salesman comes, send him to me. The LPG gas will be a clean way of cooking. No kerosene stoves will be needed."

Usha said, "If it is so good then I will take it also. Another salesman came yesterday and he was selling what he called pressure cookers. He demonstrated one and my mother in law thought that its continued hissing was because of some witchcraft. I also thought that it may burst and hurt us."

Aina said, "When new things come, people are afraid. But all things are not dangerous."

Usha said, "Yes, my sister in London tells me that they have bought a television set in which they can see many programs. It is a box in which they can hear like the radio and see like the films. Isn't it fascinating?"

"What is this world coming to! I am happy with my world. I love hearing the radio. I can't understand how all those lovely songs come out of a box. I always wonder how films and coloured photographs are made. It seems like magic to me. How do they do it?" said Bijli.

As the conversation paused, Laila started teasing Sanad. He said to Usha, "I asked your husband if he would come with me to see a movie and he said that he had to ask you."

Usha said, "No way. He does what he wants."

Laila said, "No, he can't stay away from you. He is a henpecked husband."

Sanad replied, "No. I am not. Actually Heera is a henpecked husband."

Aina quickly looked at Heera to see if he had felt bad, but Heera was laughing. He said, "Men are always supposed to be masterful and autocratic. So when I give an equal position to my wife, I am called henpecked. But I don't mind. My self esteem is not obliged to keeping up appearances. I don't need to suppress my wife just to show that I am assertive. Aina is equal to me."

Laila clapped and said, "Well said Heera! Aina, you are lucky to have such a mature man in this brute-infested world, where dictatorial men are appreciated."

Usha took this opportunity to tell Sanad, "You should be a husband like Heera."

Sanad scowled and started walking away and Usha sighed, "Now I have had it. He will sulk and make life miserable for me. He has such a king size ego."

Laila caught Sanad and said, "Sanad, tell me the answer to this puzzle. How can a person become blind if both his ears fall off."

Sanad stared at Laila and replied, "What nonsense! What connection do the ears falling off have with eyesight? Laila, you always ask ridiculous things."

Laila said, "But listen to this. A young man was staring at the doctor he had gone to consult. The doctor asked, "Why are you staring at me?"

"You have such huge ears and they wobble as if they could fall off any moment," said the young man.

The Doctor replied, "What if one of my ears falls off? What would you do?"

"Tell me which ear will fall, the right or the left?" "The right ear," answered the Doctor.

"Then I would have to walk to your left ear so that you could hear me," answered the young man.

"Very true. What if both of my ears fell off?"

The young man spoke confidently, "Then you would become blind."

"What? Blind? How would that happen?"

"You can't see without your spectacles. When your ears fall off how will you wear your spectacles? So you will become blind," explained the young man.

Aina, Bijli, Usha and Heera started laughing.

Sanad looked miffed. Laila said, "Sanad, do you know that the young man was very much like you."

"Who was the young man?"

"Sheikh Chilli." Sanad did not like it and he just walked off. Usha asked, "Who is Sheikh Chilli?"

Laila replied, "The actual Sheikh Chilli is still a mystery, but he symbolizes any individual who is 'simple' and foolish and not complexed by the brain at all. There are many jokes about him."

Usha exclaimed, "You called my husband Sheikh Chilli. That means you called him a fool."

Everyone froze as they thought that Usha had felt bad, but she burst out laughing and actually clapped her hands with enjoyment, saying, "Laila, you are really witty. What an apt description! But he is sulking, so I must go and try to appease my own dear Sheikh Chilli."

Chapter 18

The next day they were in the courtyard when they saw Sanad and Usha. Laila shouted out urgently, "Sanad, come here. I have something to tell you."

Both Usha and Sanad came quickly, thinking that it was something important that Laila had to say.

Laila said, "I have another incident to tell you about your role model, Sheikh Chilli. Once, he was sitting with the doctor enjoying the pleasant weather. It was raining. An old man came and said, "I saw the most amazing thing today. It was raining at the front of my house but the back of my house was totally dry."

The doctor agreed, "Yes, Nature can be very strange sometimes. I saw that on one side of the road it was raining but on the other side of the road it was dry."

Not to be left behind, Sheikh Chilli chirped in, "You both can't beat this. Once it was raining but I was dry above my waist and wet below."

Aina, Usha and Heera started laughing, but Sanad said, "What is there to laugh about? How can a person be dry above and wet below."

Laila just said, "When Nature takes a call."

And then Sanad understood. He said irritatedly, "Why do you tell me Sheikh Chilli jokes?"

Laila pacified him, "I was just teasing you. This is not a Sheikh Chilli joke. It was something that was said by us when I was with my friends. Now hear this. You will like this limerick.

'A lady of Niger
Smiled as she rode on a tiger
They returned from the ride
With the lady inside
And the smile on the face of the tiger.'

Sanad finally smiled at this limerick and Laila said to Sanad, "At least you are normal. You do smile, even though it is a belated reaction."

Usha said, "We wanted to invite you all for dinner."

Sanad said, "My uncle's friend Ramaasray and his wife are coming tomorrow and he is from Najapur. All of you come because I would like you all to meet him."

The next day they got ready and stepped into Sanad's house. Laila had not come with them. He had promised Sanad that he would come later. Usha welcomed them warmly and they all sat down. Only Ramaasray came out because his wife wasn't well. Sanad then introduced Ramaasray to them. Ramaasray acknowledged their greetings but he started staring at Bijli. Suddenly Ramaasray said, "Aren't you Bijli?"

Bijli became quite still as she looked at the man, but she replied, "Yes, I am."

"Sanad, why did you call such low people? Don't you know that she is a nautch girl?"

"Uncle. Don't insult my guests," said Sanad.

Aina spoke up then, "How do you know, Mr. Ramaasray?"

"I saw her there when she came to the house of Mahavir Chandra."

"How do you know Mahavir Chandra?"

Ramaasray said, "I lived in a village owned by him. I had come to meet him and he had invited me for the party in the evening. She had come to dance there."

"So that means that you went to see her dance. So you are the one who should be ashamed."

"In those days there was nothing wrong in watching prostitutes dance."

"So there was nothing wrong in her dancing there also. Why are you disparaging her?"

Ramaasray said, "It was a status symbol then for men."

"It is always correct for men but wrong for women. How unfair! But now it is considered wrong for men too to watch dancing girls. I wonder what your wife will say when I tell her."

Ramaasray said, "No, don't tell her."

"So don't say anything to Bijli also. She is my mother and I am not ashamed of her. She is such a beautiful person that I admire her. By the way, Mahavir Chandra was my grandfather. And Sanad and Usha, if you have a problem with all this, then we will go home."

Sanad said, "No, Aina. You stay. I apologise on behalf of my uncle."

Ramaasray also apologized and then they sat down for dinner. Just then Laila came and Ramaasray nearly threw a fit. "Sanad, you have called an eunuch!"

"Yes, he is my friend. And if you have a problem, you can go from my house," said Sanad.

Ramaasray did not go. Then Usha laid the dinner which was an extremely quiet affair with Ramaasray being uncomfortable and disgruntled. Only Laila was his cheerful self, but he had been so touched by Sanad's loyalty, that he did not make fun of Sanad.

CHAPTER 19

Usha also joined College to do her graduation and it became easier for Aina and Usha to go together to College by rickshaw. They went regularly but gradually, Aina felt shy as she slowly became heavier and her pregnancy became very obvious. But she did not leave her studies. She was also thankful that the due date was well after her examinations, so it would not intrude.

Everyone looked after her. Bijli was a big help. She took over the care of the household, she did all the cooking and she also looked after Khushi. With that she continued with her music classes. Heera made it a point to take Aina for walks so that she would remain fit and healthy. Laila also was very helpful and contributed by helping Bijli with the household chores.

Usha would make it a point to cook nutritive dishes for Aina. If Aina felt like eating something, Usha would be the first one to get up to make it. Usha and Sanad had slowly become very close to the family.

Aina also prepared Khushi for the coming of her little brother. She told Khushi, "Your little baby will be coming after a few days. The baby is coming for you because you are all alone. I love you a lot but we will have to love your little baby too. In the beginning baby will really be tiny and we will have to be careful."

Life went on in its busy routine, till Aina and Usha gave their exams. Then it was time for Aina's delivery.

One evening Aina felt her pains coming. Thankfully Heera was in the house. Soon Usha also came to help Bijli pack up for their stay in the hospital.

Heera used the telephone to call the taxi driver Rajan, but Rajan was out of station. Heera knew that it would not be sensible to take Aina on a cycle rickshaw, but he had no choice. So he went out to see if there was a rickshaw which was free. He did not see any rickshaw, but he noticed that a young man was parking his car in the compound of one bungalow across the road.

On an impulse, quite opposed to his inherent reserved nature, Heera ran up to the young man and said, "My wife is expecting. Her labour pains have started. Could you take us to the hospital in your car."

The young man promptly answered, "Ofcourse."

They took Aina to the hospital and Heera thanked the young man. "Flight Lieutenant Ranjit Singh at your service. I am in the Air Force. All the best."

Heera thanked him and soon Aina was in the Labour Room. It was a very difficult labour and the whole family, Sanad and Usha stood fretting with tension till they heard the cry of a baby. When Aina was taken to the ward and the baby boy was put in her lap, she saw that Heera had brought Khushi to see the baby.

She gave the baby to Laila and she took Khushi in her lap, so that Khushi did not feel that the baby had usurped her place in the lap of her mother.

Aina discussed with Khushi and then they named the baby Prasan, because both their names 'Khushi' and 'Prasan' meant 'happiness'. Everyone liked the name. Aina came home with Prasan and then life in the house was a tizzy. The usual routine was totally upset as everything now revolved around little Prasan.

Heera distributed sweets to all the people they knew. Heera also remembered to take a box of sweets to the house of Flight Lieutenant Ranjit Singh.

"That day I did not even tell you that my name is Heera. We have been blessed with a baby boy. I also want to thank you again for helping us that day."

"Congratulations and you are welcome, Heera."

"I hope not. I already have two children, so I wouldn't like to increase the population more."

"Sorry. I didn't understand that."

"See when you say 'You are welcome' then it means that give me the chance again, and again I will help you. So in this case it would mean that my wife becomes pregnant again and we trouble you again to take us to the hospital. And I am not ready for that."

Ranjit burst out laughing and said, "That is a good one. I like you."

"So do I. Are you alone here? Are you married?"

"My parents live here as they own this house. My younger brother is studying in a hostel. By chance I have been posted in Chakeri in Kanpur, so I am here with my parents. I am not married yet."

"Why ever not? You are so handsome and kind. I am sure any girl will be lucky to marry you."

"Thank you. No one has said that to me except my mother and I thought she was partial to me, so I never believed her. But I feel like believing you."

They talked with an easy camaraderie and that proved to be the beginning of a friendship that became very dear to both of them. Ranjit came to see the child and he also gifted a lovely fluffy blanket to Prasan.

Aina too liked him. They visited each other because Ranjit's parents Sharda and Baldeo too were very lovable. They asked Aina and Heera to look for a girl to marry Ranjit with. The two families started having a lovely time together at least once a fortnight.

One day Heera came and told Bijli, "Ma. A war has started and our Prime Minister has given us the slogan 'Jai Jawan Jai Kisan' (Hail Soldier Hail Farmer) which has become very popular. He has also said that on one day in a week, we should not have grains so that the financial problems of the country are less and food is sufficient for everyone."

Bijli and Aina strictly followed this every Monday during the war. Aina even did a charity programme in College for the collection of funds for the soldiers.

The war continued and then Ranjit was called to the border area. Aina and Heera tried their best to be with Ranjit's parents Sharda and Baldeo as much as they could. Everyday they would hear the news bulletin, dreading to hear Ranjit's name in the list of fatalities. And then one day, they heard what they had dreaded. They heard the All India Radio news bulletin and the announcer took the name of Flight Lieutenant Ranjit Singh in the list of casualties.

His parents received a telegram informing that Ranjit's plane had been shot down by the enemy. The plane had caught fire and fallen in enemy territory, so there was no hope of Ranjit being alive. Sharda and Baldeo faced this very bravely. Aina's respect for them went up, when she heard them planning that their younger son should also go into the Armed Forces.

Bijli also commented, "It is this emotion that keeps us Indians safe in our houses while the jawans (soldiers) suffer so much. We are truly blessed that we have families like these."

Heera said, "When we are so affected by Ranjit's death, his parents must be shattered, but they show so much dignity. It is really commendable."

CHAPTER 20

After bombing the area successfully, as he sat in the plane, Ranjit thought, "I must evade these ack ack gunshots. Oh dear! My plane has been hit. The tail has caught fire. I must eject myself at once. I hope the parachute opens up. I don't have much time. The fire will eat up the whole plane."

Ranjit ejected from the plane. Within minutes the plane went up in flames and fell downwards. Ranjit thought, "I must be careful that I don't fall into enemy territory or they will never let me remain alive. I must fall over the border in my own land."

But when he fell, he did not know if it was his own motherland or not. He thought, "How strange this is! The topography is nearly the same yet the two countries are against each other. What a pity! Just in case it is enemy territory, I must hide the parachute at once, so that no one comes to know that I am in their territory."

Ranjit looked around and then he folded the parachute quickly and kept it under some bushes. He took care that the parachute was not visible. In the distance he saw smoke coming out. "That means there are some people in that area. Let me go and check if I am in enemy territory or in my country."

He ran towards the smoke and some distance away, he lay on the ground and started crawling so that nobody could see him. "I must take all precautions if I want to be alive." And then he saw the army tents some distance away. "Oh dear! I am not in my own country. I have fallen in enemy territory. I have to be very careful."

After he realized that, he started crawling again. He kept away from the tents and then he stopped. He took his bearings and then he turned towards what he thought was the east. He started crawling again, hoping that he had taken the right direction. Suddenly he heard footsteps. He froze and he even tried to still his gasping breathing, because the footsteps were coming closer.

He ducked his face down and pressed himself against the ground, so that he would be covered by the grass and bushes around. The footsteps seemed to be coming right towards him and when he felt that they would certainly detect him, the footsteps turned away towards the right and the men walked off.

After five minutes, he dared to breathe freely again. He was so shaken by this, that he felt he couldn't move, but then he thought, "What if the people come back again? The footsteps seemed to be of the heavy type, probably army boots, so they must be soldiers. It is dangerous to stay here."

He forced himself to move on and keeping the smoke on his left, he moved forward. He went on, and after about an hour, he felt that he couldn't go on. He was thirsty and hungry. His body was aching and now he could feel a terrible piercing pain in his right hand and realized the excruciating pain meant that there was a fracture. He tied a piece of a branch to his right forearm.

Then he just lay down limp and turned on his back. He saw the sky, tinged by the setting sun. How beautiful it was but how ugly was, what the people had made of it. He waited for sometime. Probably he slept because when he next opened his eyes, it was twilight. Again he turned and started crawling towards the east. He refused to feel thirst, hunger or pain as he chanted in his mind, "I have to reach my motherland."

The whole night he moved and then rested, trying to put his ears to the ground for the sounds of footsteps. He felt night change into dawn and then the sun came peeping out. It was so beautiful, yet it increased his danger because in the sunlight, he could be seen easily.

Still he kept crawling the whole morning and he again took his bearings. He tried to keep alert except when his body gave way. Then he rested under some bushes, as the sun became too hot to bear. He started again when he could tolerate the sun.

After that it became more of a reflex action because he was not aware in between what was happening. Throughout the night he rested when his body gave up and then he moved. As the first light of the day dawned, he suddenly felt a shock. He was right near an enemy camp. He thought, "I better move away fast before the soldiers get up. I better be careful of the soldiers who would be guarding the enemy camp."

He saw a guard only some distance away. He was in two minds. "If I move, he may hear me and if I don't move, he might walk towards me and see me." Ranjit stayed where he was and he thanked his stars for that later, because two more guards came up and started talking to the first guard. Ranjit bided his time and then he gradually lifted his head and saw that the guards had not moved. Suddenly a man called out to them and they started moving towards that man.

In a trice, Ranjit got up and ran as fast as he could. He was taking a chance because the man who had called the other guards was facing him, but he banked on the fact that he would be shielded by the other three guards. The moment he came near the bushes, he dived and lay flat on the ground.

"That was a close shave," he thought, trying to quell his breathing and palpitations.

The whole day he moved with a frenzy, only stopping when he couldn't move. He forced himself by telling himself, "I can do it. I will not die in the hands of my enemies. I have to escape."

That frenzy gave him the energy to go on till the No Man's land between the borders. He wept for joy, but then told himself, "Don't be emotional. I have to reach my side of the border and then only will I be safe."

Now he had to be really careful because there was more possibility of patrolling soldiers. "It will be very tragic if I am killed right near the border of my country." So he kept waiting under some bushes, till he saw some soldiers march past. Then he started moving.

It took a long time for him to drag his body to cross the wire and then he was in No Man's Land. He stood up with his shirt and waved towards the guards on the Indian border. Finally they sighted him and helped him and he collapsed as soon as he thought, "Ah! I have reached my motherland. I am safe!"

He was taken to a military hospital and after a week came a telegram to the parents, that changed the tears into smiles. Ranjit was still alive, but it was only after a month that Ranjit returned home. By that time, the only injury they could see was a fractured right arm.

They all were there to welcome Ranjit and he told them what had happened. "I was not scheduled to be on the flight to bomb the enemy, but the officer who was to go, became sick and there was no one else to replace him. I went in the plane and bombed the targets, but then anti aircraft guns started firing at me. I saw that my aircraft had caught fire. The few seconds that I got to eject out, probably saved my life."

"Where did you fall?" asked Heera.

"I fell in enemy territory. I then took my bearings so that by mistake, I wouldn't go deeper into enemy territory. My judgement proved right and I moved towards our border. And I did not stop for food or water.

I don't know how I managed it. Probably my yearning for seeing my motherland was so strong, that I went on. It took me three days and nights to reach our border and that was the happiest sight of my life. Then I was in hospital and because the war ended, they let me return home. The happiest part is that we won the war."

Great were the celebrations on his return but soon life came into a regular routine. Aina was immersed in the routine, but her keen observation made her notice that Khushi had started sulking a lot. Aina realized that this was because everyone else was besotted with Prasan. So Aina one day talked to the others.

"Listen, I know that a baby is always more lovable, but we should make sure that Khushi does not feel neglected. The baby is too small. He will not realize whether we are giving him time or not, but Khushi will certainly feel ignored, specially as till now, she has got everyone's undivided attention and affection."

After that, they all made sure that they would play with Prasan when Khushi was in school, but once she came home, they would focus on her only. Khushi soon forgot her sulks. She was very happy that her little brother was a baby who had come just for her. She was very loving towards Prasan, and Aina felt relieved.

CHAPTER 21

Heera got a job of an accountant at the shop of Bala Seth, a jeweller and everyone was happy at home. Heera soon got immersed in his work and tried his best to do his work well. But he soon realized that Bala was not being honest with his Income Tax and Sales Tax returns. Bala Seth would bribe the officers and tamper his account books. Heera confronted him with it, but Bala Seth was brazen about it, "What is the great deal about it? Everyone does it. What is wrong with my doing it? I am not tampering with your money."

"You are cheating the government and that indirectly affects all the citizens. It is wrong. It is an offence. I will not let you do it. I will tell the officers what you are doing," replied Heera.

"Then get lost. You are fired," yelled Bala Seth, and Heera walked out.

Heera got two more jobs, but the same thing happened again and Heera walked out. He now knew that he couldn't continue in jobs, because some where or the other, he would see that illegal things were being done and then he would leave the job. It was ironic that his employers wanted him to be honest in his work, but they wanted that he should let them be dishonest.

He got quite disgusted with the state of things and he started thinking that it was better not to do anything under anyone else. So he started thinking that doing a job or service was not a good idea as one had to kowtow to a boss. He started thinking of professions where he would be independent. So he thought that he should study to be an advocate. For that he wanted to study law which was a two year course. He worked out that his finances would last out till he finished his law.

By this time, Aina and Usha finished their graduation. Usha got a second division but she did not feel jealous of Aina who had passed with a First Division, having scored 66% which was a great achievement. Everyone felt very proud of Aina.

One day Aina was sitting with her mother and Bijli asked, "What will you do now?"

Aina knew that it was difficult for Bijli to manage the house, her music classes, Khushi and Prasan. Though they had admitted Khushi to a Nursery School, there was still a lot of attention that Khushi wanted.

So Aina said, "I will stay at home and look after the house and the children."

Bijli said, "Is that why you had done your graduation? I know that you want to study more but you are not thinking of studying more, because I will have to do everything in the house alone. But I insist Aina that you should study more and get as many degrees as you can. You must study enough to get a steady job. I am able to manage at home and I quite enjoy it. I will feel good that I am giving you the opportunity to study more. Rather I will feel bad if you don't study more."

"All right Ma."

Bijli said, "Aina, none of us want to deprive Khushi and Prasan of love and attention, but we should work as hard as we can to achieve something in life."

So when Heera told Aina that he was thinking of joining law, she also decided to study law with him. But Aina felt that she should also do her masters. So she joined the Master of Arts course in English, which had morning classes and she went with Heera to her law classes in the evening. It was very tough for her to study for two degrees, as well as manage Khushi and Prasan.

Heera and Aina would go together to study law. They had separate bicycles and they went for evening classes. Aina was the only girl in the first year of the law class. The classes were from six in the evening to ten in the night but such was the desire to study, that Aina braved her fears and rode her bicycle down with Heera from their home till the Law College. Part of the road was very lonely and often the streetlights would be off because of power breaks. Both of them put an iron chain with a lock on one end, on the bicycle handle, to use for defense in case someone troubled them.

One day they realized that a motorcycle was following them. Heera came abreast of Aina's bicycle towards the roadside so that Aina was on the side of the pavement. Heera said, "Aina, a motorcycle is coming behind us with the rider and one man pillion. I think we are being followed by them. I will face these people if they try to trouble us. Don't wait here like a simpering movie heroine. Remember that you have to pedal hard and ride home fast in such a situation and get help."

Aina heard the drone of the motorcycle coming nearer and her heart was in her mouth with fear. Then she took a deep breath, but her fears seemed to be so inflamed that she had palpitations. Closer and closer came the motorcycle and now they were level and just as Aina thought that she would faint, the motorcycle rode on and went ahead. Aina got a glimpse of the rider and the pillion rider and she started shaking so badly, that she felt she might fall off her cycle.

Heera sensed that something was wrong, "What is the matter Aina?"

"Heera I recognize the two motorcyclists. One is Babu and the pillion rider is Raka. They are criminals and they have been known to commit a murder."

"How do you recognize them?"

"One day when I was doing my graduation, they were standing at the College gate. My classmate pointed them out to me and told me to be careful of them. These two always remain together and they are dangerous."

"Oh dear! Come on hurry up. They might come back, so pedal faster so that we reach home quickly."

She sagged with relief when she reached their lane, but Heera did not let her relax. Heera said, "We will be safe only when we are inside our house."

Thankfully the motorcycle did not come back and they finally reached without anything untoward happening. When they told all this to Bijli, she said, "Heera, why don't you buy a car? The risk would be less. Nowadays it is not safe to be on the road in the night.

Aina and Heera were shocked the next evening to see that Babu and Raka had also taken admission in their Law college, and they also noticed, that these two were after Aina.

Heera did not take any immediate action. He started greeting them normally whenever he met them. Then he started stopping to talk to them in a friendly manner. He was very pleasant in his behavior and did not show any animosity.

Then one day he introduced Aina to them. He told them that she was his wife and that they had two children. Aina talked very politely to them and they did not have the courage to say anything to her. After that Aina maintained her dignity and kept a distance from them, but she wasn't standoffish towards them.

Somehow this ploy worked and Babu and Raka did not trouble Aina. Moreover Babu and Raka left the law course. After that they never followed them.

CHAPTER 22

Heera used to take Khushi to school in the morning because he was free then, as law classes were in the evening. He would take a law book and sit in a park near the school and study, because after two hours he had to bring Khushi home.

One day a middle aged man sat down next to him. When Heera looked up from his book, the man said, "My name is Vijay Nath." Heera told his name and then Vijay Nath asked, "What do you read all the time?"

"I read my law books. I am a law student."

"I work in a bank. Can I ask a favour of you? I come here for a walk. I sit here for fifteen minutes and then I go home because I have to reach my bank. The fact is that I have no one at home. I am completely alone and so I feel very lonely. Can I talk to you for those fifteen minutes everyday? If you don't feel like it, you are free to refuse. I won't mind that."

"No, Mr. Nath, I don't mind at all. Rather I will like it if I can talk to you for fifteen minutes or more."

"Oh good! That takes care of the week days. I will not be lonely on week days. Now there are two problems. One. You call me Vijay, and not Mr. Nath."

"That can be remedied. I will call you Vijay."

"The second problem would be the Sundays."

"Vijay, you can always come to my house and meet my family on Sundays."

"Or you all can come to my house. Oh! That is lovely! By the way, I hope you didn't mind my asking this favour. But the Sundays together will only materialize if your family agrees."

"I think they will agree with pleasure, Vijay."

Heera had agreed because he felt that it would be churlish to refuse, but he was dubious whether he would like talking to Vijay daily, but it turned out that he enjoyed those conversations and soon the two became great friends. Despite the age difference, they got along fine and they could be seen animatedly discussing politics, economics, social customs and many other topics. Heera started looking forward to meeting him. So in the morning Heera would drop Khushi, talk to Vijay and during the day he would help Bijli at home and study, and in the evening, were their law classes.

Vijay often came on Sundays, and Sanad and Usha would also join them. They would all sit in the courtyard and listen to the stories that he told Khushi. He would also recount incidents from his past. He became very attached to Khushi and Prasan and would always bring chocolates for Khushi. One day Vijay Nath asked Usha, "Why do you look so sad always?"

Usha did not reply but just walked away. Aina then said, "Usha has not been able to have a child and her mother-in-law blames her for it and calls her barren. This really hurts Usha and lately she has started feeling very depressed and sad."

Vijay said, "Aina, I love to think that things have changed, but they really haven't. In the past also women were blamed, like Usha is being blamed. Nothing has changed. I wonder when narrow and orthodox attitudes, old conventional beliefs and bad social customs will change. I only wish that people change soon. Only education can bring about this change. I am so happy that you are studying so much."

Aina said, "You are right. Education is very important, specially for women. Education alone can change public awareness by enlightening people."

Vijay was a very helpful person. He helped Rajan too. The tonga driver Rajan had realized that there was little scope for tongas being used any more with the advent of taxis and buses. So he had sold his horse and tonga and learnt driving.

Rajan met Vijay Nath at Heera's house and he asked him whether he could get a loan to buy a car, which he planned to use as a taxi. He was helped by Vijay to get the loan and then he bought a car. So now Rajan had become a taxi driver. Heera felt that Rajan would know about cars, so he asked Rajan to help him decide on a car. Heera then bought an Ambassador car and he was very proud of his purchase. He would take Khushi and Aina for a drive whenever he could. Now it was easier going to the Law college in the car.

Time went by in a whirr and Aina and Heera both passed their two year law course. Aina passed her MA examinations. Heera and Aina discussed their future and Aina decided that she would stay away from courts and teach, because teaching would give a steady income, though with Heera, she also enrolled in the Bar and paid the stipulated money necessary for permission for legal practice.

Heera started his training under a famous advocate Dhar. Soon he was showing himself so adept at law, that

Dhar began sending him to the court also to present some cases. Finally Heera felt that he was ready to start his own legal practice. As he had already made a name for himself while working under Dhar, it did not take him long to get work. He was taking up criminal cases, and he enjoyed getting his innocent clients freed from the accusations and from punishment.

CHAPTER 23

The family also felt very happy when they saw the progress that Laila had made. When he had stood up for Naren, people had been impressed by his oratory. Moreover it was because of his fiery oratory that all the workers had unified and the factory management had had to surrender in front of their unity.

Seeing this success, soon, the trade union leaders started calling Laila whenever there was some problem in some mill or factory. So it could be said that people had finally accepted Laila. Laila had changed his name and now people knew him as Lalla Kumar.

The fact that Laila was more relaxed was because he had started accepting the fact that people would comment on him. He often said now, "When I am an eunuch, people will call me an eunuch, isn't it? Now I don't feel bad about it." So Laila accepted himself and the people accepted him as an eunuch, though there were odd instances when people did manage to get under his skin and wound Laila, like it was in his first major Trade Union speech.

The workers of a mill had gone on strike and they had called Laila but the moment he had gone on stage, a section of the people had started chanting, 'Eunuch. Eunuch.' Laila had tried not to react but then another Union leader Birju Lal came onto the dias and when he saw Laila, he said, "I will not share the stage with a damned eunuch. Tell him to go, then only will I sit on the stage."

Laila felt very upset at this public humiliation but then one section of the workers started chanting, "Lalla Kumar. Lalla Kumar." This chant was taken up by others and soon the crowd was booing Birju Lal and cheering Lalla Kumar. Finally Birju Lal had to leave and Laila gave his speech to a cheering crowd, who were thrilled by his oratory. And then there was no stopping Laila.

Gradually Laila was spending less time at home because of his commitments outside with the Trade Union. They all missed the gaiety that Laila had always spread in the house, but they were happy that Laila had found something to do which was slowly turning into a vocation, and which was giving Laila happiness.

He had always wanted to achieve something and now he started feeling that he was doing something worthwhile. Sanad missed Laila the most. Though Laila had always teased Sanad and Sanad had always reacted as if he was miffed, still there was an affection that had grown between the two. Usha also loved to cook the favourite dishes of Laila.

One day Usha's mother-in-law Pushpa came to visit Sanad and Usha. Pushpa was a widow who generally stayed with her elder son who had not married. Pushpa was very critical of Usha and whenever she came, she made life difficult for Usha.

Now she had started telling Usha to divorce her son because she was barren. In the late evening, they heard Pushpa shouting, while Usha was crying. "Leave my son so that I can get him married again to a girl who can give me a grandson."

Bijli could not stop herself. She knocked at their door. Sanad opened the door and Bijli could see the irritation on his face, as he said, "My mother keeps shouting. She just doesn't stop. I don't know what to do."

"Don't worry, I have come. I will talk to her," said Bijli.

Pushpa said, "Why are you coming here? This is our family matter. Why are you intruding?"

Bijli replied in a firm but polite voice, "If you shout so much and don't let the neighbours sleep, then it is not a family matter. Then it becomes a matter for the neighbours. Why are you shouting so much? Why can't you just discuss your problems without anger?"

Pushpa said, "How can I think of discussing, when my daughter-in-law is barren and there is no son to carry our name forward? How can I keep quiet?"

Bijli replied, "How do you know that it is the fault of Usha? It can also be the weakness of Sanad."

Sanad seemed offended, but Bijli went on, "I think both Usha and Sanad should go through medical tests to see if they can have children. Then only should you rant and accuse Usha."

"There can be nothing wrong with my son," said Pushpa.

"All the more reason that you get the tests done and stop this blame game you play every time you come. You are making life hell even for your son and daughter-in-law by telling them that Sanad should marry again so that he can have a baby."

Next day, Bijli literally forced Sanad and Usha into getting ready. Aina took them to the doctor. There were a series of tests and then the doctor told them that

Sanad was impotent. Sanad was in a state of shock but the effect on Pushpa was devastating.

First she ranted that Aina must have bribed the doctor to give a wrong report. Then Pushpa took Sanad to another doctor, but the result was the same.

It was a very subdued Pushpa who talked to them the next day, "I was wrong. Sanad is impotent. Now there will never be a son to carry on our family."

Aina said, "Ofcourse, there can be. Why don't Sanad and Usha adopt a child?"

This met with a vehement refusal from Pushpa but after a long persuasion, she finally agreed. Pushpa had to go back to her elder son who had gone down with fever. Sanad took Usha to an Orphanage and they chose a baby girl who was very cute. Pushpa returned to Sanad's house after some time and started on her spree of shouting why they had adopted a baby girl and not a baby boy, but Sanad said firmly, "Ma. I wanted a daughter. After some time, we will adopt a son too."

But Pushpa would not even look at the baby.

One day Bijli told Sanad and Usha, "When the baby cries, you both come out. Be a bit callous and let the baby cry. Then we shall see what Pushpa does."

So that day, when the baby started crying, Usha and Sanad stayed in the courtyard. Pushpa was alone inside their house. She heard the baby cry and she tried to ignore it. But when the baby went on crying, Pushpa started calling, "Usha, Sanad. Where are you both?"

But when both did not turn up, Pushpa went and stood next to the baby. Then she could not stop herself. She picked up the baby in her arms and that was the moment she became a slave of the little baby. After that she could not have enough of Chikki, as they started calling the little baby.

Pushpa was totally enamoured with her granddaughter and she started staying with Sanad and Usha longer, so that she could be with Chikki. The redeeming fact was that now Pushpa was kind towards Usha and life seemed to be better for the whole family.

One day Chikki was in her pram and they were sitting in the room sharing dinner. Laila said, "I think that I will start match making as a career. The first marriage I will fix is between Chikki and Prasan. What will the two parents give me as a reward?"

Heera and Sanad started teasing each other, when suddenly Prasan got off his chair and walked to Chikki. Then he bent down and kissed Chikki.

Heera burst out laughing as he said, "Laila, you will get nothing, as my son will just run away with Chikki himself. You were just talking, but he has showed his intentions himself."

CHAPTER 24

One day when Aina went to meet Ranjit's mother Sharda and father Baldeo, she found Sharda crying, "Aunty, what is the matter?" It turned out that Ranjit had told them that he loved a girl Rita who was not of their caste. Sharda said, "We don't have a problem with the intercaste marriage but Rita is not the type of girl who will mix with our family. We all are homely people and she is too modern. But Ranjit is adamant and he will not listen to reason."

Sharda and Baldeo had to agree to the marriage because it came to a point that they would have lost Ranjit who would have separated from them and married Rita. Aina and Usha helped Sharda with the marriage preparations. Aina and Usha took part in all the rituals and customs and Sharda considered them as a part of her family.

Rita's parents were also not in favour of the wedding. So it was decided that the wedding would be done from home and then there would be a Reception in the Air Force club. Just the family members were present during the wedding rituals.

Ranjit's wife Rita was educated and modern and Aina was slightly dismayed how Rita was not as shy as a bride should be. Rita was quite bold and was deciding things herself and was at times overruling the decision of her mother-in-law and her husband. Rita decided what she would wear and what would be the decoration and arrangements at the Reception. But Ranjit seemed quite happy with her as if she could do no wrong.

But Aina was pained to see that Sharda Aunty had to give in when there was a clash of opinions and that Ranjit sided with Rita all the time. Then a Reception was given. Heera and Aina loved the sophisticated ambience at the Reception with the muted music and elegant decoration. The guests were also very dignified and on the whole, the Reception was good.

The wedding passed off beautifully, but Aina and Usha were aware how unhappy Sharda and Baldeo were. They never showed their pain to anyone but in their hearts of hearts they had started feeling that their elder son Ranjit was lost to them forever, as he would kowtow to his wife only. But Ranjit was unaware of the suffering of his parents, though he loved them a lot. The only problem was that he loved Rita the most now and he had blinkers towards the sharp tongued Rita.

When Ranjit had taken Rita for a honeymoon, Aina went to help Sharda with the left-over work of the wedding and that day the pain welled out and Sharda cried. She said, "She is the wrong girl for Ranjit. He is too straightforward and simple. She will really twirl him around her little finger. Rita insulted me so many times. Aina, does education mean that a girl should not have respect for her elders? You are also educated. You don't disrespect elders. Aina, Rita will break up my family."

Aina had felt the same herself but she tried to console Sharda, who said in the end, "I think we were better off in the past where the youngsters always were obedient and respectful towards elders."

Aina said, "Aunty, there is nothing wrong with education. It is how one uses the education. An educated person should be able to bind a family together more than an illiterate. I think that being modern does not mean that one should disrespect elders and only do what one wants."

"Aina, I wish I had a daughter-in-law like you."

It was six months later that Ranjit invited his parents to his house in Poona where he was stationed. Ranjit said on the phone, "Ma, you and Papa should stay with us now permanently. Why should you stay alone in Kanpur? Come and spend time with Rita."

Sharda and Baldeo did not want to go, but then they thought that Ranjit would feel bad if they didn't accept his invitation. They went prepared to stay for a long time, but they returned within a fortnight.

Sharda told Aina, "Rita made our lives so miserable. She wanted us to go according to her dictat. She did not want us there permanently, so she saw to it that we returned. Do you know Aina? In a way we have been chucked out of our son's house."

Aina said, "But didn't Ranjit say anything Aunty? He had invited you."

"Rita did not know that Ranjit had invited us. You know how simple Ranjit is about all this. So when she came to know that we were to stay there for a long time, she threw a tantrum saying that she did not want her freedom curbed because of us old fogies. She forced Ranjit to get train tickets for us. And the fact is Aina, that I am glad we didn't have to stay there. We were so uncomfortable in our own son's house. Now we will never go to Ranjit's house."

Aina remarked to Heera later at home, "How can girls behave like this? Can't they realize how hurt the parents feel? Or are they so selfish that they are ready to be ruthless and uncaring."

Aina and Heera made it a point to go often to meet Sharda and Baldeo, so that they would not feel lonely and uncared for. Specially on festival days, they tried to include them in the celebrations so much so that one day Baldeo said, with tears in his eyes, "Aina and Heera, you both look after us so well and make us feel so loved when you are not even related to us. But my own son and daughter-in-law don't even care to send a greeting card to us on festivals. God bless you both."

CHAPTER 25

On the professional front, Heera got the first major case of Radhey, who was a landlord from the rural areas. Radhey had a lot of money and his father came to Heera and said, "Don't worry about the expense. Just get my son out from this case."

Heera asked, "Is he really innocent?" and he was assured by the father that Radhey was innocent. Heera started preparing for the case in all earnest. He would come and discuss the case with Aina and soon Aina was totally involved in the case.

Aina said, "The murder happened in the Tora village on the fifteenth, but Radhey was in Lucknow on 15th. How do you know that this is true?"

"Three people have vouchsafed for this and they are willing to testify in court under oath. The troublesome point is that the murder weapon hasn't been found. We don't know what case the Prosecution will put up but I need to be prepared for every eventuality. What we do know is that a man called Takla was stabbed with a sharp instrument and his dead body was lying near the haystack. Takla was a moneylender, so this murder could have been done for money. But Radhey is a wealthy man. Why would he kill Takla for money?"

Aina said, "Is Radhey married? What about Takla? Was he married?"

"Yes Radhey is married and Takla has left behind his widow and five children. Radhey had never seen Takla's family."

Aina said, "Then Radhey has no reason to kill Takla. And you say that Radhey's father says that the villagers saw the poor farmer Birju near the dead body."

"Yes, so it is very possible that Birju killed Takla because he was not in a position to return the loan he had taken from Takla. It is an open and shut case."

"Somehow Heera, I feel uneasy about this poor farmer Birju being so expediently seen near the dead body. Wouldn't he have run away if he had killed Takla?"

Heera stated, "But all the facts point to Birju."

The next day Aina went and sat in the courtroom as the case against Radhey started. Radhey stood proud and unflappable and totally unrepentant. Aina did not like him.

She thought, "I am getting negative vibes about Radhey." But legal cases were not fought on instincts or vibes. After the routine questions and answers, the Prosecution brought a police constable on the witness stand and to the chagrin of Radhey, they produced the murder weapon. It was a long, straight rod, pointed at one end. The Prosecution lawyer thundered, "So this was the weapon you found near the dead body of the deceased."

The constable agreed, a trifle too hurriedly, "Yes, your Honour."

Aina was looking at Radhey and she saw a look of fury flit across his face and then he beckoned Heera, and Aina who was sitting closeby heard him say, "The police are lying. This is not the murder weapon. Just imagine. The constable is telling lies. The murder weapon was an axe."

"But how do you know?" asked Heera.

"Oh lawyer, don't be daft. I myself threw the axe in the middle of the deep pond the other side of the Tora village."

Heera stared at Radhey. He turned around and looked at Aina. She just looked back at him and nodded. He got his answer. He stood up and said to the judge, "My Lord! I withdraw myself from this case. Please catch Radhey and send him behind bars because he is the murderer. He has just told me that he had thrown the axe he had killed Takla with, into the pond."

Radhey was livid. His supporters and his family were shocked. They shouted at Heera, "How can you do this to your own client?"

Heera said, "This is a court of law where justice has to prevail. I cannot free a murderer and get an innocent man to the gallows."

"We will not pay you even a paisa."

"Thank you, because I can not accept even a paisa from a murderer." Heera and Aina then left the courtroom. All Aina did was press Heera's hands and say, "You did right. I am with you. I am very proud of you. I love you." They went home.

After a few days Aina's lawyer Uncle, Sabal came to meet them. Heera told him about the dishonesty prevalent and Sabal answered, "It is everywhere Heera and one has to live with it. You have to make compromises to survive in this cut throat world."

"I can't make compromises with honesty."

Sabal said, "Then get into Income tax or Sales tax and leave criminal law."

"Is there honesty in these disciplines?"

"People make all sorts of adjustments to save tax."

Heera said, "Then I cannot represent them."

"In this way you will never be able to earn money."

Heera said, "So be it."

"Why is your house so cold?" asked Sabal.

Heera said, "A building has been constructed right behind our house which blocks the sunlight. Now there is no privacy because the people in the flats can look down at us all the time."

"Why are they spoiling the quiet beauty of this place near the river Ganga? It is a pity but construction has started in many areas in Lucknow also."

Heera said, "There are just too many people. The houses are not enough for them."

Sabal got up to go. He said, "Where is your mother, Aina? I would like to meet her before going."

Heera said, "She must be in the courtyard behind. You can come there."

They walked through the rooms to the courtyard behind and Sabal met Bijli very affectionately. All at once rupee notes started falling down on them. They all looked up with surprise. They saw the people in the flat of the topmost floor of the building emptying suitcase after suitcase of money which was raining down at them. Finally the rain of currency stopped.

Bijli asked, "What have they done?"

Sabal explained, "Income Tax officials must be raiding their house. They must have thought it better to throw all the money down rather than be caught with it."

Sanad and Usha also stood gaping at the money dropping as rain. Sanad laughed, "Heera, all your financial problems for your life time have been solved by this rain from heaven. Lucky you! I have never seen such a lucrative rainfall before in my life."

"Come on, help me in picking up this money."

They all got together and picked up all the money and they kept it in a big trunk. Sabal asked, "What will you do with all this money?"

"Return it to them," replied Heera.

Sabal joked, "But you can keep it all because this is all black money."

Heera was very sure when he said, "All the more reason not to keep it with us."

Sabal said, "Do you know? When I see you Heera, I feel that there is hope for our country."

Sabal went away and that night when the owners of the topmost flat came down for their money, Heera and Aina returned each and every rupee to them. Even those people were surprised.

CHAPTER 26

Heera also became very particular about the cases he took up. He would see to the best of his ability that the people he defended were honest people. Many were the cases that he refused because they had some element of deceit in them.

Aina supported him in whatever he did, though their savings were fast depleting. He earned erratically and so both of them decided that Aina should join a teaching job so that regular income could come to sustain their everyday expenses.

The rounds of schools and colleges started and it was frustrating to go from one institution to another without success. When she tried in schools, they wanted the Bachelor of Education degree, so privately Aina filled up the form and decided to do B. Ed. with her teaching assignment, if and when she got a job.

In some schools they said, "We will give you less but you will have to sign on a larger amount. If you are ready, you can join our school."

Ofcourse, she wasn't ready. She had her values in place and so it was another round of applying for jobs and giving interviews where often the interviewers would be making disparaging remarks about her name. She was quite disgusted with the scenario but she persisted.

For some days she worked in a small school on a temporary basis for Rs. 150 only. After the stint finished, finally, she was able to get a job in a degree college, but alas! her salary was all of 426 rupees only. She was delighted at getting a job, but disappointed at the meagre salary, but teachers were paid very low salaries and nothing was being done about it.

What was missing in terms of money was made up by the adulation she got from her students and colleagues. Though she was young, she had the knack of managing the students very well and after some days, it was a regular feature that as she entered the front gate of her College, she would see a row of students on either side giving her flowers. The row extended right till the Staff room where her colleagues would wait for her.

The moment she entered the Staff room, they would take all the flowers and pin them up on their hair and leave the best blossom for her.

After a month, the Head of Department said to Aina, "You are an ornament for our English Department."

And then things looked up when Heera came charged with enthusiasm and told Aina, "I have got the case of a man who has been caught for killing his driver. Do you know who my client is? Surjit Singh. He is the wealthiest man in the city. I went to the jail to meet him. He looks very decent."

Heera studied the case and discussed it with Aina. Heera explained, "The police had found Singh with a gun in his hand while he was lying unconscious near the dead body of his driver Lachchu. The police is saying that Singh killed his driver Lachchu and then playacted as if he was unconscious because he could not run away before the police came."

"Why would Singh kill a driver?" asked Aina.

"The police say that Lachchu was blackmailing Singh about his affair with his Accounts Manager Yunisa. Singh had got most of his property and wealth from his wife Farzana. He did not want Farzana to know about his affair, so he killed Lachchu."

"What did Singh tell you?"

"Singh is saying that Yunisa killed the driver Lachchu because he had come to know that Yunisa had bungled accounts and committed fraud to the tune of twenty lakhs. Just after the killing, Singh walked in. Yunisa then hit the gun on the back of Singh's head. She then cleverly put the gun in Singh's hand when he became unconscious and she ran away."

"What is Yunisa saying?"

"She is denying everything. She is saying that she is innocent. She is saying that she neither had an affair with Singh nor did she bungle accounts. She is saying that she hadn't gone to the office as it was a Sunday. She is saying that Singh is into drugs dealing and he is just making a scapegoat of her by fabricating these stories, as Lachchu is no longer alive to refute what Singh is saying."

"She may be right."

"But then Farzana also suspects that her husband was having an affair with Yunisa."

"Maybe she is being a typical wife. Most wives, except me, suspect their husbands."

"Thank you for not suspecting me."

"You are welcome. But how will you prove that Yunisa could hit Singh on the head?"

"She is the daughter of a wrestler and she has learnt wrestling from her father."

"That doesn't prove that she hit Singh."

"She is quite broad boned and tall. She seems quite capable of knocking down a slim man like Singh. You know that rich people and celebrities are often more vulnerable than the ordinary people. Maybe she is taking advantage of that."

"Maybe not. I am not convinced. And she doesn't seem to be the type of person Singh would have an affair with. But these are my instinctive feelings. I think that Singh is framing her. The situation has made her seem a sitting duck. The circumstantial evidence is fragile. You see how the cross questioning goes. Why was Singh there on a Sunday?"

Heera said, "I asked him. He said that Lachchu had told him about the account bungling, so he went."

"When it comes to his defense, Singh is taking the name of Lachchu who cannot ratify what Singh is saying because Lachchu is dead. Very clever!"

"Will you come to the court tomorrow?"

"I have an assignment I cannot postpone. I won't come to the court but later on I will come to your chamber. All right, now go to sleep so that you are fresh for tomorrow."

As soon as Aina reached the chamber, she came to know that Heera had won the case. She was just able to congratulate him, when Singh walked in with a buoyant step. He was overjoyed and he thanked Heera profusely for winning the case. Then he took out his cheque book and said, "Tell me any amount and I will give it to you."

Heera said slowly, "Before I take money from you, just tell me one thing and please be honest about it. Did you murder Lachchu?"

Suddenly Singh was sombre and quiet; and then he said, "Yes."

Coolly Heera got up and he pointed to the door of the room and then in a calm voice he said, "Get out."

"But your fee. What should I fill in?"

"Stop it. I don't want your dishonest money. I will not take a paisa from you. Get out of here."

Singh was still his cocky self as he walked out, but with a studied precision, Heera took the hand of Aina, pulled her towards the front door of the room and walked out. He turned around and put the lock on the door, never to return. But he did go to court once more, when the case against the innocent Yunisa started.

Without taking any fee from her, to atone for his sin of getting her into the clutches of the law, he defended Yunisa and thankfully got her freed without any blemish added to her name. He also apologized personally to Yunisa.

And that was the end of the legal career of Heera.

CHAPTER 27

Aina supported Heera when he stopped his legal practice, but she became more anxious about how they would manage the growing expenses of the house. She increased the rate of her tuitions from fifty rupees per month to seventy five rupees, though she was always afraid that the students may stop coming for the tuitions. Bijli too had more children now to learn music. Aina made Bijli promise that the moment the music classes became a burden, she would close them.

Another thing bothered her. She saw that her family members were again favouring Prasan who would get away with extreme naughtiness. If they fought with each other, Khushi would be scolded but everyone would leave Prasan scot free with the corollary, "Oh! He is the younger one. Let him be."

She sat down with everyone and made them aware of what they were doing. She told them that Khushi could get a complex and may even start resenting Prasan if this continued. Aina also told them not to make Prasan win in all the games he played, because then he would get used to winning and that would make him unable to bear the failures that might assail him in his future life.

So the behavior of the family became more conducive to a healthy development of Khushi and Prasan as from that time, everyone was careful not to favour either child. Aina was happy with the changed attitude of her family members. Soon there seemed to develop a strong bond between the siblings.

When Khushi went to school, Prasan would start crying that he too wanted to go to school. So Aina bought a school bag for Prasan. Aina explained what happened in school to Bijli, because Bijli had never gone to a school. So when Khushi went to school, Bijli would play 'School, school' with Prasan. She would make him draw, play games, learn the alphabets as if he was really doing them period-wise in a school. But everyday Prasan would cry that he wanted to go with Khushi.

So one day Bijli told Aina to get Prasan admitted in school. Aina talked to the principal who admitted Prasan to school. Now Prasan was also going to the school in the Nursery. He loved playing in the sand pit the most and he would take his playing blocks to make mud pies. He loved making different things with the plasticine that the teacher gave the children. He also loved to colour with his crayons. Soon the walls of the house were also used by Prasan to show his drawing and colouring skills, much to the chagrin of the elders.

Bijli started getting more free time. Bijli took this opportunity to start learning with the children. Both the children were quick learners and Bijli would learn with them. Aina was satisfied with the academic progress that Khushi had made in the second class and Prasan in the Nursery class.

CHAPTER 28

Heera started looking for another job. The children had started going to another school. Both had been admitted to the same school, so Heera no longer went to the park where he had spent so much time with Vijay Nath. But when he did not get a job and things were not working out, Heera felt like meeting Vijay Nath.

Vijay Nath saw Heera sitting on the bench where they had always met and talked. He understood that Heera had specially come to meet him. He sat down and said, "You are looking very tense. What is the matter? Tell me, I might be able to help you."

"I have stopped my legal practice. I cannot support lies and deceit." He told the details of what had happened in the court.

"So you are worried about what you will do now to earn money."

"That is right. I know I will not get a job and actually I don't want to do a job. I always found it very oppressive to listen to the orders of a boss, specially when the orders included doing unethical things."

Vijay said, "I have a suggestion to make. Our bank wants us to finance more projects. If you can get a viable project, then you can apply for a loan. I will see to it that it is sanctioned."

"No, I do not want that you go out of your way to give me a loan."

"Do you have any property?"

"I have a house In Rojpur."

"Do you have some money to pay twenty five percent of the loan that you will be taking?"

"There is some money which we had kept for Khushi and Prasan."

"So, you can mortgage that property and give that money and you would get the loan easily without my going out of the way. Just get a good project."

From that day Heera began to explore projects for setting up a factory. When he talked with his family members and told them what Vijay had proposed, Laila said, "Did you hear the adage that you look everywhere in the world, but the thing is right below your nose?"

"What do you mean? Do you have a project?" asked Heera.

"You know that Sanad is an engineer. He was telling me that he has a project, but his mother is not letting him leave his job to set up a factory."

"Then I can take up the project and set up the factory and he can be my sleeping partner."

Laila became serious, "Heera. I will not allow it. Only my sister can be your sleeping partner."

Heera laughed and said, "Accepted. I would like to talk to Sanad and work on this quickly."

Just the next day Sanad came to talk to Heera with his project of a new invention that had a scope of becoming a rage. He told Heera about pocket calculators that could be made.

"This is being made abroad and if we can capitalize on it now, we may be one of the pioneers in India. I have a complete project report. I have everything ready except the finance and the fact that my mother is not letting me leave my job."

The capital needed was substantial and so Heera decided to take Vijay Nath's suggestion and apply for a loan from the bank. Heera talked to Sanad and settled the terms for their partnership and then he signed an agreement with Sanad. A lot of paper work had to be done. After that they submitted the project report to the bank. It took some time, but the loan was sanctioned.

When Vijay Nath told Heera that he had got the loan, Heera asked, "I hope I deserved to get this loan only on my own credentials, otherwise it would be nepotism and I can't accept that."

"I know that, Heera. I am not going out of my way in giving you the loan. Now stop thinking all this and start working on your project. And tonight you all will come to my house and we will have a feast to celebrate this. You must bring your mother too."

"Aina's father too has come to stay with us," said Heera.

"You must bring him along too. What is his name?"

"His name is Kalka Prasad. One thing I would like to tell you is that his wife's name is Gomti who brought up Aina."

"I understand. Aina must be the biological daughter of Bijli, who wasn't married to Kalka. It happened in olden days. Am I right?"

"Yes, you are. I think you will get along well with him. He is quite an amiable person."

Kalka had come to Kanpur to stay with his daughter Aina for the first time. Aina was very happy but the happiest was Bijli who had always loved Kalka a lot.

Bijli still loved Kalka and when he came, she started cooking all his favourite dishes.

Aina laughed, "Ma, so these lovely dishes are being made for Papa. Isn't it a fact that we always celebrate by cooking and eating? If we want to show our love for anyone, we cook their favourite dishes. The way to the heart is certainly through the stomach."

Kalka said, "I am getting my favourite dishes after a long time. I have been missing them so much. But I must say that the dishes taste the same as they did so many years back."

"See Ma, he did not miss you. He only missed the dishes prepared by you."

"It doesn't matter. Atleast he remembered me in some way," replied Bijli.

"Ma, how sweet!"

Heera added, "Aina, you should learn from your mother." Everyone laughed.

When they went for dinner, Vijay Nath got along famously with Kalka and it was a happy feast. Aina loved the open flat that Vijay had on the second storey of a building. Aina loved the open look because there were many windows and none of them had grills and Vijay liked to keep them open. A cool breeze was blowing and Aina was enjoying the view outside.

Just then Khushi came running and said, "Ma. Prasan will fall. He is not listening to me."

Aina asked, "Where is he? Take me to him."

Khushi took Aina to the bedroom of Vijay and Aina stopped. She felt petrified. Prasan was sitting on the window sill which had no grills and there was a sheer fall down from the second floor. Prasan had his feet dangling outside. He was sitting with his hands cupping his chin. Any movement and he could fall right down to the ground. Aina felt panic. She opened her mouth to scream. Suddenly a hand came across her mouth and Heera's voice said, "Shhh! Don't scream."

Aina then stood paralysed as she saw Heera walk extremely slowly and noiselessly towards Prasan. The distance seemed interminable because they were so worried that Prasan may fall. When Heera was just two yards away, Prasan looked back and Aina nearly fainted with sheer terror, but Heera inched slowly ahead, talking to Prasan, "So Prasan. Are you having fun? Isn't it very pleasant today?" Prasan smiled and nodded. By then Heera was near enough and he bent and grabbed Prasan. Everyone had collected near the door. They all heaved a sigh of relief as they hugged Prasan turn by turn. Then Bijli asked him, "What were you doing there?"

"I was seeing two birdies."

Kalka asked, "How old is he?"

"He is a little over three years old."

Vijay Nath asked, "How did he reach the window? It is quite high."

"He pushed a chair till the window and then he climbed it," answered Heera.

All the grown ups took time to get over the incident, but Prasan started playing with Khushi within seconds. He could not understand why the grown ups were fussing over him more than usual.

"Childhood is so innocent and blissful. Prasan does not even realize that he has just been saved from injury or possibly, death. That is why I love children," remarked Vijay.

"Where are your children?" asked Kalka.

They all waited eagerly to listen to the answer as they knew nothing about Vijay. He said, "I never married. I loved a girl but she was not of my caste, so my parents did not allow me to marry her. You know how it was in the past. I don't even know where she is now. All I heard was that her parents married her off quickly. I could not think of marrying anyone else, so I have no children."

Aina said, "You should not speak like this. We are your children."

"Yes, since you all have come into my life, it feels that I have got a family. You are like a daughter to me. Your Khushi and Prasan seem to be the grand children I never had. Heera seems to be the son I never had. I haven't told you all that I have cancer. I am not keeping well and I didn't go in for chemotherapy, as there was no one to live for. Now I want to live, but it is too late. Will you do one thing for me Heera? When my end comes, will you do my funeral rites?"

Heera had tears in his eyes as he nodded and they embraced each other. Aina and Bijli burst out crying. They were sombre when they returned home. Vijay Nath's condition deteriorated very fast.

The end of Vijay came just two months later. Aina and Heera were with him in his flat. Vijay Nath had seemingly been sleeping, so they had been sitting quietly next to his bed.

Suddenly Vijay opened his eyes and smiled at both of them. He then asked Heera to pick up a photograph which was kept on his bed table. Heera saw that it was an old faded photograph of a lovely girl smiling for the camera. Vijay Nath held the photograph in his trembling hands and looked at it. He rested it on his heart, patted it twice and shut his eyes. And that was it.

Aina and Heera did all the funeral rites as Vijay had wanted. They decided not to tell anything to Khushi and Prasan. Later the children missed Vijay and often asked to be taken to his flat, but Heera would distract them by taking them somewhere else.

As time passed, with the resilience of childhood, Khushi and Prasan became more attached to Kalka and soon Vijay Uncle faded from their memory.

But Aina and Heera felt a deep seated vacuum because Vijay had become a father figure to them. When Aina cleared her B. Ed exams., she thought how happy Vijay would have been if he had been alive. Heera specially missed him because Vijay had become a friend, guide and support for Heera.

Kalka too went back to Najapur because his wife Gomti was sick. The house seemed empty without him and Bijli was the most affected, but she never showed her loneliness to anyone.

CHAPTER 29

Life had to go on. One day they got an invitation for a concert in Khushi's school. Khushi and Prasan were also acting in it. The preparation for the concert also distracted the children and helped them forget Vijay Nath. In the school concert they were enacting the story of the Pied Piper and Khushi was selected to act as one of the rats. She was very excited and she insisted that all of them should come to her school for the concert. Laila refused and Khushi became very upset.

She pouted, "You have to come."

"No, I can't. I have some work to do."

Prasan also imitated Khushi and said, "You have to come."

Laila looked helplessly at Aina and said, "How can I go to their school? All the children will tease them about me. I don't want them to be ashamed of me."

Khushi said to Laila, "You have to come or I will not go to school."

Prasan also repeated it and Laila could not resist. He had to go and Aina said, "Don't be afraid. I don't think anyone will humiliate you or Khushi. The audience will have educated people who should not demean you, just because you are an eunuch."

"I don't believe you. No one will accept an eunuch to sit with them and see a concert."

143

"I think the children will be very upset if you don't come along. Don't be anxious Laila. You are wearing men's clothes, so the people may not say anything."

But still Laila was very tense. He was more tense for Khushi and Prasan, than for himself. He told Aina, "Maybe the people there will recognize that I am an eunuch because of my walk and talk."

"Relax. It will be all right," said Aina gently.

Suddenly Aina realized that Bijli was tense too and she asked, "What is the matter, Ma?"

Bijli whispered nervously, "What if someone recognizes me?"

"No one from Najapur will be there, so don't worry," she said reassuringly. Her heart went out to both Laila and Bijli for their fear of facing people.

As they reached the school and got down from their car, Aina could feel the nervousness that Laila and Bijli were feeling. She quietly took Laila's hand in hers and patted it. Heera caught Bijli's hand and then they started walking towards the hall in which the concert was being held. Laila's hands were as cold as ice.

It was the first time he was going with the family for a public event. They approached the entrance of the hall and Laila clutched Aina's hand tightly. Aina kept holding his hand and they walked towards the door. They paused at the entrance because another family was going in.

When their turn came, Heera showed their tickets which he had purchased as it was a concert for charity. The usherer was one of the teachers. She counted all of them and then said, "Please go in. Fifth row from the left." Not a single raised eyebrow. No stare. No glare for

Laila or Bijli. Aina felt Laila and Bijli perceptibly relax as they walked down the aisle.

People looked up and looked a little longer but that was because Aina was looking strikingly beautiful in her white and red sari. Some people did look at Laila a little while longer, but there was no disdain and no reaction that could be called abusive. Heera understood the anxiety of Bijli and he said, "Ma. See, no one has recognized you, so please relax and enjoy the concert. Just think about Khushi and Prasan."

And Laila relaxed too. Laila from that moment changed from being diffident, to being confident in public. In his men's clothes atleast, Laila, now Lalla Kumar, became free now of any inferiority complex about being seen even in places where the high society people came. The eunuchs also left him alone because he would help them whenever they were in trouble.

The play 'Pied Piper' started and the costumed rats jumped all over the stage. Khushi was one of them and Khushi as the little rat was very chubby and sweet. She had inherited the fair skin and big eyes of Heera. Then the Pied Piper came and told the town chief that he would take the rats away. He played a tune on his flute and the rats started following him. He took them away.

The Pied Piper then asked the town chief for money but he refused. Then the Pied Piper played a tune and all the children followed him. Prasan was one of the children and he looked very cute. Prasan had the dusky complexion and the narrower twinkling eyes of Aina. The family really enjoyed the play, specially because Khushi and Prasan kept looking at them, and kept giving them lovely smiles.

Chapter 30

Heera and Sanad hired a shed and started the factory with the loan money from the bank. Heera found that Sanad was very diligent. He did not leave his job because his mother had ordered him not to, so Sanad would do his job and then come to the shed and work there till night. Heera too worked very hard, so both Sanad and Heera developed a very good rapport. Another thing that helped their partnership was that Sanad was as honest as Heera. So they had no conflict on this count. Both of them did not like to give bribes. Slowly Sanad and Heera became good friends.

Heera was in the process of consolidating his factory when war broke out in December 1971. The war was one of the shortest wars in history. It was only for thirteen days, but they felt the impact when they saw the worried parents of Ranjit, when Ranjit had been sent to the front. Ranjit who had become Squadron leader came to meet his parents because he knew that they would be very worried about him.

Aina and Heera went to meet him. Rita had refused to come with Ranjit and in a way Sharda and Baldeo were relieved that she had not come.

Aina met Ranjit's mother Sharda and asked, "Aunty, how are you?"

"Aina, at this time I am very happy. We have won the war and God has saved Ranjit. Just listen to what he has been through."

They sat down to listen and Ranjit said, "I had to drive down to our Air base and for that we had to go through a village near the border. There were very few villagers there, as the village had been evacuated because of the war. We saw a tea vendor sitting on a platform under a tree and we got down to have tea."

Ranjit remembered the whole incident.

He got down from his jonga when the tea vendor shouted, "Sir, come and have tea. You never know if you will be able to drink tea after this."

Ranjit then started walking to the tea seller with a jawan on either side of him. He felt strange, as he had the feeling that someone was watching him. He looked around but there was nobody else that he could see.

They were standing in a clearing where there were just two trees, one under which the tea vendor was sitting and the other at a distance on the other side of the muddy road.

As he bent, his ears picked up a sound and he hesitated and looked behind. When he saw nothing, he bent down to pick up the glass of tea. Just then there was a gun shot from the other tree and the two jawans ducked. The bullet went over Ranjit and hit the tea vendor who now lay dead. One jawan hissed, "Sir, that was meant for you. Let us move fast."

They turned around, but in a trice, the jawan on his right shouted, "There is a sniper in the other tree," and the jawan pushed Ranjit away. As that jawan was now standing where Ranjit had been, the bullet that had been shot at Ranjit, hit the jawan. Before Ranjit could do anything, the jawan on his left side, fired a shot at the other tree, and they heard a scream and saw an enemy sniper fall dead, from the tree across the road.

Ranjit said, "Both the bullets fired by the sniper had been meant for me, but they killed the tea vendor and one of my jawans. I was saved, but I still feel guilty that two people died instead of me."

The conversation veered to other subjects and Aina started teasing Ranjit about having children. He sobered down a bit and said, "I want to have children but Rita says that having a child will spoil her figure. She also says that a child will be a big bother. Aina, are children a big bother?"

Aina answered, "It is a fact that having children is something that changes your life, but then you stop thinking about yourself and think only of the children. So you don't mind the change in your body or lifestyle. You have to be selfless, so that you can devote yourself entirely to the children."

"But Rita is not ready, though I have told her that we will keep an ayah for the child."

Heera said, "It is so ironic Ranjit that Usha wants a child but cannot have one, while Rita can have a child but doesn't want one."

"Yes, you are right. I know that my parents too would love to be grandparents, but Rita is just not ready to listen to me. I feel quite frustrated with her. She is very stubborn. We have started having massive fights often because I want to have children as I adore children."

"She has a very strong will," said Aina.

"She is selfish and wants me to be a henpecked husband always. She is only happy when I agree to whatever she says, otherwise she is rude. I think that I have made a mistake by marrying her. I realize that she tries to keep me away from my parents too."

This was the first time Ranjit had said something against Rita, and Aina looked at him with sympathy in her eyes. Ranjit stayed a fortnight with his parents and had heart to heart talks with them. He came to know how unhappy Rita had made them. He faced upto all facts honestly and after becoming aware of the actualities, in that fortnight, he decided to divorce Rita.

As soon as the divorce came through, Sharda and Baldeo arranged a match for Ranjit and married them in a quiet wedding in Delhi. The name of the bride was Abha and she was known to Sharda and Baldeo.

Aina and Heera met them after a year and by that time they had been blessed with a baby daughter. Abha was a very good daughter-in-law and mother. She also looked after Ranjit very lovingly and now Ranjit was very happy. He looked ecstatic as he played with his beautiful baby daughter whom they had named Lavanya.

CHAPTER 31

Setting up the factory was very traumatic. It took a long time for everything to fall into place. Heera and Sanad worked really hard but they needed more help. There was no one to help Heera in the running around in getting the formalities done. When Heera went out of the factory, there was no one to manage the factory.

Laila was busy with his Trade Union activities. Moreover Laila did not want people to laugh at Heera that he had an eunuch as a brother-in-law. Sanad had already told Heera that he couldn't leave his job, so he couldn't be there during the day time.

One day Aina said, "Ma, Heera is working all alone. Laila is not free from his commitments all the time. I will go and live in the factory during my holidays."

Nothing anybody said, could change her mind. The children insisted that they wanted to go with Aina. Bijli said, "You can take Ramu with you to cook food." Heera had forced Bijli to keep a servant. Ramu had come to work for them and he had turned out to be an extremely reliable person.

"But Ma, then you will have to cook food here?"

"I will manage. Only Laila and I will be left here. It won't be a lot of work."

So during her holidays, Aina went to live in the factory. They converted a room in the factory into a bedroom and she moved in there to stay. They fitted out a kitchen and Ramu cooked for them. It was convenient because Aina could manage the office while the children played in the room. Moreover, Heera could now go out of the factory without worrying about it.

One afternoon, they went back to their house for Bijli's birthday. They enjoyed the feast cooked by Bijli, but then Sanad came and said, "Heera, I have heard that there are dacoits near your Panki estate. Do you cross the road which goes under the railway track?"

"I cross it everyday when I have to come to the city," replied Heera.

"Be careful. Just yesterday in the evening, a factory owner had been ambushed by dacoits who had been waiting on the other side of the underpass. They took all his money, his ring, watch and gold chain and when he tried to resist, they shot at him. He is in the hospital with a gunshot wound."

Bijli became nervous, "What is happening to this world? Crime is increasing everyday. Heera, all of you better go home fast and when you reach the factory, you must call me on the telephone."

Bijli pestered them to go early, but it was dark when they were a couple of hundred yards away from the underpass and then the car stopped. Aina and Heera looked at each other in panic.

"Oh Heera! What will we do now? It is so lonely here."

"We cannot walk to the factory as it is very far away still. There are no petrol pumps or car mechanics here. We cannot do anything. But if we remain in the car we will be like sitting ducks for the dacoits. Let us get down and walk back to the colony that we passed on our way. Thank God, the children have gone to sleep."

They got down and locked the car. Heera took Khushi in his arms and Aina carried Prasan and they started walking back. It was a long road and they trudged along. Both the children were quite heavy and so they were soon tired. They walked quite a distance and then they saw the colony, but it was totally dark. Then Heera sighted one light and they started walking towards it. They reached the house and saw that there was a light inside the house. Heera knocked at the door and a man looked out cautiously. Heera said, "Our car has stalled. Please help us."

It turned out that the man was a doctor who had just come back from a night visit to a patient. He was kind enough to take Heera to the petrol pump some kilometers away. Meanwhile his wife looked after Aina. She put out a cot for Khushi and Prasan and then Aina rested her weary arms.

The doctor knew where a car mechanic lived. He woke up that man and got him to set the car right and then Heera drove the car to the doctor's house. The doctor said, "You are lucky that this did not happen a little later because dacoits come at this time. Now you may beat them to it, but if they attack you, just don't stop even if they come under the car. They are very ruthless."

Heera thanked the doctor and his wife and then they started for the factory. As they reached the underpass, Heera said, "Aina, bend and hide yourself. I don't want them to see you." He at once pressed the accelerator as much as possible and the car zoomed through the underpass. Soon they were beyond it.

Heera did not lessen his speed. They hurtled on and Aina straightened up and looked behind. She shouted,

"Go faster Heera. There are many people there. They are running after us." Suddenly something hit the car from behind.

"What was that?" shouted Heera.

"They have thrown a long stick at our car."

That made Heera take the next bend in the road as fast as he could. They were nervous till they finally reached their factory. Heera got off and saw the long dent on the car which was made by the long stick thrown at them by the dacoits. Heera said, "Aina, you and the children should not stay here in the factory. It is not safe. There are only factories here and there are no women or children staying here."

"If you can live here, we can too. I am not going to leave you here alone, atleast till I have my holidays. What we will be careful about is, that we will try to avoid going out at night."

Aina called Bijli and told her that they had reached safely. She did not tell her mother what had transpired, because she did not want her to be worried about them.

Aina and Heera kept on working hard. After a week, Aina woke up in the night feeling very uneasy. She felt that something was wrong. She strained her ears. Everything was very quiet and suddenly she stiffened. She had heard the shuffle of feet. She quickly woke up Heera and whispered, "I think that there are some people outside. I heard the shuffle of feet."

Heera quietly went to the window and looked out from the chink in the curtain. He made out some outlines of men outside, stealthily walking towards their door.

Heera said to Aina, "I think there are many people outside. They must be dacoits. I can see one person with a gun. Let us act as if there are many people in the factory."

Actually, only Heera, Aina, the children and Ramu were in the factory at that time, but Heera told Aina, "You don't speak. Keep the children quiet. If the dacoits come to know that a woman is here, they might be tempted more to attack us."

Thankfully the children were sleeping. Aina kept sitting there to see that the children wouldn't get up. Meanwhile Heera put on all the lights and checked that all the doors were bolted. He woke up Ramu and apprised him of what was happening. Then he started shouting names as if many people were there.

"Ramu where are you? See if the machine is working properly. Hari, you must complete the production tonight. All of you should complete the scheduled production even if you have to work till 7 in the morning. Mohan, make tea for the workers, so that they don't feel sleepy. This important consignment has to go tomorrow."

After some time, Aina felt as if she had heard a shot being fired. She went to the window and peeped out from the chink, but she could not be sure. Throughout the night, Heera kept all the lights open and they didn't sleep. Heera and Ramu kept rods near them, just in case the dacoits managed to come in. When the light of dawn touched the factory, Ramu and Heera looked out of the windows and became convinced that no one was outside. Then they all relaxed.

When they saw the police arrive in one of the factories across the road, they sent Ramu to find out the reason. Ramu came and told them, "Yesterday ten dacoits had entered that factory. They shot at the guards and they stole everything valuable there. One guard is seriously injured."

Heera went out to meet the policemen. They confirmed the news. When Heera came back, Aina and he went around the factory. They saw that many feet had trampled the newly made flower beds. Even the flower pots were disturbed.

Aina said, "So there were ten dacoits outside our factory in the night. Heera, your presence of mind probably saved us from them. Don't tell Ma, or she will not let me stay with you."

"I also think that it is not safe for you to stay here, Aina."

"I can't stay without you. If you stay in the factory, I will stay here," said Aina.

Heera said, "Khushi is ten years old. She is growing up. I don't want anything to happen to her. You also look young and attractive. There is danger from the workers too because most of the workers leave their wives in their villages."

Aina replied, "I will explain things to Khushi. I will tell her how to protect herself."

Nothing that Heera said, would make Aina change her mind, but then one day she wished she had gone back home. That afternoon while having lunch, Prasan fell down from his chair and there was a gash on the back of his head. He started bleeding and Khushi tried to stem the blood with anything she could get her hands on.

Heera shouted, "We must take him to a doctor."

Heera quickly started the car and he drove like a maniac while Aina sat with a towel pressed to stop the bleeding. There were no doctors near the factory. They went on driving for quite some time before they saw a market. Then they could not find any doctor because all the clinics were closed. Aina sighted one clinic which was open. They rushed to the doctor who had his own family in the clinic. The doctor attended to Prasan and finally the bleeding stopped.

The doctor said, "You found me here because my son Sunny has lost my car keys."

Aina said, "Thank you Sunny for losing the car keys because that saved my son Prasan."

Heera paid the doctor and he and Aina thanked the doctor. Just as they were about to drive away, the doctor found the car keys in the car. He himself had forgotten to take out the car keys from the ignition.

CHAPTER 32

The next day Heera went to Delhi to meet his distributor and some suppliers. Aina sat alone in the office. The workers had just gone home after working the whole day. Only Ramu was there in the factory. Aina had put Khushi and Prasan to sleep.

Just then a group of eight people entered her office. The team leader said, "We are from the Electricity Department. We have come to see whether you have paid the bills regularly." He had the audacity to just pass her table and sit down on Heera's chair.

Aina said, "We have paid all the bills. Why are you all crowding round in the office?"

"Dutt sahib, we will wait outside," said one of the people of the group. But Dutt did not get up. He told Aina, "Show me the Electricity Bills."

Aina showed him the bills. She knew that everything was in order, but Dutt said, "You have to give me five thousand rupees, otherwise we will cut your power connection."

"Why should we give money if everything is in order?"

"See Madam, there are so many loopholes in the rules and regulations, that I can get the power cut on any count. So it is best that you pay up five thousand."

Before she could answer, Dutt picked up the phone without asking her permission. He started calling the other factory owners and Aina was flabbergasted that he was asking for money from all of them. When he told the Factory owners to bring the money to Aina's factory, Aina could not bear it.

She stood up and said, "I don't know how you can blatantly ask for bribes in this manner. I will not pay anything to you. And I will not allow you to call all the people here to take a bribe. If you have to do this, go some where else. You can't force yourself here."

"Madam, I can do what I want, but you are a lady, so I will go to another factory. But let me tell you one thing. I will give you just five days. If you don't pay up till that day, your electricity connection will be cut."

"We will do what we think is right and you do what you think is right, but not in my office."

Dutt flounced out of the office, saying, "I will come after five days."

He walked out, leaving a very pensive Aina behind. She was thinking that they were at a crucial point because they had to deliver an order. If the power was cut, Heera would not be able to complete the delivery and then it would be a major setback. They might have to close the factory.

She was so deep into her thoughts, that she started with surprise when she heard Laila say, "What is the matter Aina? You are looking very worried."

"Laila, how have you come here?"

"The workers of a factory are on strike and they called me. I thought it was a good opportunity to see how you all are. We really miss you and the children. Now tell me why you are worried."

Aina told him the reason and then said, "The electricity should not be cut or we will not be able to complete the manufacturing schedule. But I know that Heera will not be ready to give a bribe to Dutt. And if Dutt does not get the money, then he will cut the line."

"Why don't you give the bribe without Heera knowing about it?"

"Even if I did that, we don't have money. Laila, I want you to do one thing."

Aina told Laila, "Ma has my jewellery. Take the gold set and go to the jewellers and ask its worth."

She had to persuade the reluctant Laila who then went to do what she had asked him to do.

Laila then called her and said, "Aina, the set is worth six thousand and twenty rupees."

Aina was shocked, "Is that all the money for such a heavy set?"

"All the jewellers I went to, calculated and told me the same amount."

Aina said, "I got a call from Heera. He is coming back from Delhi tomorrow."

The next day Heera returned from Delhi. He asked Aina about what had transpired in the factory. She told him about Dutt asking for a bribe.

Aina said, "I thought that the bribe should be paid, so that the electricity will not be cut."

Aina was not prepared for Heera's reaction. He was livid. Aina had never seen Heera like this.

He glared at her and shouted, "Why did you pay the bribe? You should not have given the bribe. Go away. I don't want to have anything to do with a wife who gives bribes. Both giving and taking of bribes are sins."

"Dutt would have cut the electricity and then you would have had to close the factory."

"Aina, you should have let the man cut the electricity connection. I would happily have closed down the factory. But this I will not tolerate. By the way, where did you get so much money to give the bribe. When I went, you had just fifty rupees in your purse. How did you pay five thousand?"

"My jewellery set was worth six thousand rupees."

Heera just flopped on his chair and he held his head with his hands in a gesture of defeat. And then he shook himself and said in a level tone, "I am so angry with you, but I realize that this is also a sacrifice on your part. But it is just misguided sympathy. You should not have paid the bribe."

"All right, relax. I was just sounding you out. I have not paid the bribe," said Aina.

"And did you sell the jewellery set?"

"I never said that I had sold it. I just said that, 'My jewellery set was worth six thousand rupees'. But Heera, if you want, you can sell the jewellery."

"No, I will not sell your set. Why did you tell me that you had paid the bribe?"

"I did not say that. I just said that 'I thought that the bribe should be paid so that the electricity will not be cut'. How can I give a bribe when my husband is such an honest man?"

"Good girl! Now let me start my work. I want to employ two more workers."

Aina said, "But Heera how will we pay them?"

"Relax Aina. I went to our distributors and they have given me an advance that should see us through these troublous times. Once our lot is sold, the profits will get us out of this financial mess."

Aina told Heera, "The man Dutt from the Electricity Board said that he would come after five days. He said that if we didn't pay up till that day, then the electricity connection of our factory will be cut. What should we do about this?"

Heera said, "Let us wait for Dutt to come. I will deal with him."

But Dutt never came after the five days probably because the Emergency had been enforced in the country. Dutt may have been afraid of the repercussions that could happen if he took a bribe.

CHAPTER 33

When the children's school re-opened, Aina came back home. After that Heera devoted himself to work totally. It seemed that he worked all the time. He would go early in the morning and come late at night. Aina understood that Heera needed to work hard to make a success of his factory, but she was also worried that Heera looked tense all the time.

Working to face and surmount the hiccups in setting up the business and making it profitable, were understandable, but soon Aina realized that Heera had become a workaholic. The time came when the factory was doing very well as the profits were good. They had paid up their loan and Heera was able to sell his house in Rojpur. They had money now, but Heera still worked all the time. Something snapped inside Aina and she started feeling depressed and out of sorts.

She told Heera, "Why don't you relax and enjoy the fruits of your labour?"

"You don't understand. In this line, there is cut throat competition now. If I don't keep one step ahead of them, then I will lose the advantage. I have to work."

"Why are you after money?" asked Aina.

"I am not after money but you have to admit that money is never enough. I have to work for solid savings so that we never feel financial insecurity."

And then one day, Sharda Aunty came and said, "Is everything all right with your marriage, Aina? You should keep tabs on Heera. I saw him with a lovely lady. They were laughing and having a good time in the car."

"Aunty, if you are trying to say that Heera is having an affair with someone, then don't worry. I am very certain that Heera will never cheat on me. If he would be having an affair with someone else, he would be honest and tell me. Moreover I don't think that Heera can have an affair with anyone. He loves me too much."

"Your faith in him consoles me," said Sharda.

And Aina told herself, "I have full faith in Heera," but somehow the visit of Sharda made her feel more depressed. She decided that she would not let this fester inside her as a grudge. So Aina said point blank to Heera as soon as he came back home, "Today Sharda Aunty came to tell me that she had seen you with a lovely lady. She thought you were having an affair."

Heera seemed to freeze, and then he asked, "What did you say?" Aina looked with alarm at his face which had suddenly flushed a deeper shade of red.

She said, "I told Sharda Aunty that you loved me too much to have an affair with anyone else."

"My wife is always right," said Heera, but Aina heard a false note in the forced gaiety in his reply.

She still told herself, "I trust him." Yet during the next days, her dejection increased and she also felt bone weary. It became a problem for her to go to teach. She would sit in her verandah and look out at the bridge over the River Ganga.

The sky was grey with heavy clouds and grey was reflected in the water. Only the white lights of the bridge in the distance dispelled the gloom, but she felt that there were no lights in her life because she was troubled about Khushi and Prasan too.

Aina had thought that Khushi had been quite sorted out when she came into her teens, but when Aina became depressed, Khushi started throwing tantrums. Khushi and Prasan also started fighting between themselves and Aina was often irritated by those fights.

Then one day she heard them quarrel. They were using the words that she used herself when she was angry, and she realized that she herself was the culprit. She was taking out her frustrations by being angry and the children were simply imitating her.

She called the children and talked to them and said, "I have started shouting a lot. Now I will try and curb my temper." They promised to control their tempers too, but the rhythm of the house remained disturbed.

Then Aina said to Bijli, "What is this life? Why do we live? It seems a punishment and nothing else."

"Aina, life means to face challenges with the ultimate aim to discover our potential and to cherish the precious gifts we are blessed with. Till we reach the final destination, life should be devoted to the pursuit of truth. We should just happily face life as it comes, taking one thing at a time, with honesty as a companion."

"Ma, it is so difficult to be happy."

"Aina, you are unhappy because you now get no attention from Heera. You grudge the time Heera spends on his work. But you love him. Don't you want him to be happy? If his happiness is in his work, then accept it."

"Ma, can't he keep a balance between his family and his work? Why should the woman adjust always?"

"Because we women can adjust. We are made that way, to give. Because we are basically mothers who can even suffer extreme pain to deliver children, but men are wired differently. They are less emotional so these things don't occur to them. So a woman should adjust."

"Now I do nothing but keep waiting for him."

"Aina, I waited for your father when he could be free from his wife and family. You have to give Heera space. See his good points. Heera never surrenders to failure, but fights on. He sticks to his values and says, 'I will not leave honesty'. You are lucky to have him."

Aina said, "I do appreciate him, Ma. But I do feel that he should change. I feel very lonely."

Bijli said, "It is very difficult to change anyone. Habits are hard to change. Instincts are hard to change. Come on. Become emotionally strong. Make yourself self sufficient. Help your children become mature. You need to look after them, rather than think of loneliness."

Aina replied, "I want to, but how?"

Bijlee replied, "Your mind is a slave of your will power. You can make the mind do anything you want. Tell your mind what to do and trust that implicitly, then your mind will carry out your orders."

When Bijli walked away, Aina faced herself honestly. She realized that she was playing a martyr and carrying a grudge against Heera that she had been so supportive towards him always, but he had put a blind spot towards her. She stilled her mind and put the affirmation in it that she could manage alone and that she would always be there for Heera. She wanted him to be happy, because she loved him.

Then she made herself count her blessings. "I have my children, my parents, my brother and Heera. I don't want anything more." After that she felt happier.

After a week, Heera came to her and said in a very serious voice, "Aina, I have to talk to you."

Aina felt frightened. His tone seemed so ominous. What was he going to say? Was he really having an affair? Did he want to leave her? Aina's thoughts ran riot and then Heera said, "Let us go for a drive." Aina looked at him in amazement because it was ages since he had suggested a desire for her company. Heera forced her into a car and started driving.

Aina felt numb as the car moved through the traffic. She was in a daze. She thought, "How will he tell me that he wants a divorce? What should I reply?"

"Aina, we have reached our destination. Now get down."

Aina looked at the huge spacious house amidst a beautifully planned garden.

"Whose house is this?" asked Aina.

"Yours." It took time for that one word to seep into her brain. Heera made her take the house keys and open the front door. He took her from one room to another, silently. And then in a gentle loving voice, Heera said, "Do you like your house? Are you happy?"

Aina just looked at him and then she threw herself at him. They twirled around the rooms, from one room to another like two mad adolescents freaking out. Then they stopped and they looked at each other.

Heera asked, "What would you like to call your house?"

"You should say 'our house'. Call it what you had said as you stopped the car. Our Destination."

"May I welcome you to Our Destination, milady?"

Aina's answer was not audible as their lips met and sealed their love. Heera said softly, "Thank you for trusting me despite what Sharda Aunty said."

He kissed her again and muttered, "The lady in question was the architect who has planned this house. First I thought I would ask you to plan the house, but then I wanted to give you a surprise. And it was worth it. Are you happy with the house as it is?"

"Very, very happy. I wouldn't have it different," whispered Aina, caressing his hair lovingly.

"You can plan the interior decoration."

"Thank you, we will do it together. But I have one objection, milord. You talk too much."

And then naturally the house was silent except for the pent-up heartfelt expressions of love.

CHAPTER 34

It was a happy year when they shifted into their new house. It was made happier when Heera was given the Best Entrepeneur Award. They all were delighted. They left the children at home and only Aina attended the function with Heera in the Merchant's Chamber. As Heera walked to the stage to accept his award, he caught Aina's hand and took her to the stage.

Aina was moved to tears as Heera accepted the award and then in his 'Thank you' speech, he said, "I owe this award to the unflinching support given by my wife Aina and my family. I have learnt from her to go on striving and to never give up."

Photographs were taken and everyone congratulated Heera and Aina for the award. When he came back home, Heera gave the award to Khushi and Prasan and said, "This award is for both of you, as I could not give you time when you needed me the most."

"Thank you Papa," chorused both the children.

"What does this award make you feel Papa?"

"It makes me feel that I should work more and that I should remain honest always. This award gives me a sense of responsibility that I have to maintain myself on the right path, without making compromises. And this is what I want from my family and from you children. Many people are dishonest and there are wrong things being done. But despite all that, I want you to be honest and true always, and to work hard to achieve your goals and do your country proud. Promise me!"

Khushi said, "We promise Papa. We will work very hard and we will always be honest and truthful. I want to be like you and Ma when I grow up. You both don't spare yourselves. You go on working and you never give up. That is why despite so many problems, you are successful today."

Heera said, "Ma and Laila, this award is also for both of you. If you had not stood by us and managed the house, Aina and I could not have achieved anything. I am always without worry about the children and Aina, because I know that you both will look after them. Thank you so much."

In the privacy of their bedroom, Heera caught Aina in an embrace and said, "I have really made you suffer. I admit that I have become a workaholic. Aina, I need to work. I enjoy work. But I love you and the children also. Thank you for bearing with me. Thank you for being there for me always. I promise that now I will try to balance my profession and my home life. I have not given you and the children time. Now I will make it a point that you and the children will be my first priority."

The next day a photograph came out in the newspapers of Heera accepting the award with Aina by his side. At once Aina became scared. Heera noticed it and asked her, "Why are you scared? You should be happy that we have received such a prestigious award."

"Heera, I am happy but I am scared because I don't want anyone to know that we are in Kanpur. Rocoo must have completed his sentence. He must be out of prison. Maybe he wants to take revenge from us."

"Aina, you are right. I had become so busy that I had forgotten the existence of Rocoo."

"And maybe Maakhan is still looking for us."

"Aina, why would Maakhan look for us?"

"To take revenge. Don't forget that I had thrown hot oil on him. I don't think that he could have forgotten and forgiven that."

"Aina, you are worrying uselessly. I don't think that they would like to commit another crime which could take them back to prison."

Aina kept quiet and Heera again became busy. But Aina could not quell the fear that she felt. She tried to forget her fear and for that she started thinking of pleasant thoughts. She thought that she had much to be thankful about.

After such a long time, life had become good. They had enough money not to be bothered about the immediate future, and the success of Heera's business gave them hope that the future would rake in quite a lot more money. After such a long time, they finally had their own house, which they had furnished very well.

She loved her new house. They had made the front room into a drawing room and behind it was the dining room. Till then they had always eaten sitting on the floor in the kitchen, but they now had a dining table and chairs. The kitchen was spacious and had the latest gadgets, like an imported mixie and electric oven.

They had servants but Bijli still enjoyed making some dishes off and on. Money had made life easier certainly and atleast the insecurity about money had gone from Aina's mind. There were separate bedrooms for everyone and two guest rooms too.

Aina loved the fact that her father Kalka had come to stay with them permanently. His wife Gomti, who had brought up Aina, had died and so, Kalka felt free to spend the remaining years of his life with Bijli. Aina felt happy to see her biological mother and father together again. Bijli had never been happier and it was a pleasure to hear her hum in the kitchen as she cooked some favourite dish for her beloved Kalka.

And then Aina had a lovely idea. She talked to Laila and Heera and gave her suggestion. "Let us get Ma and Papa married."

They all thought it was a brilliant idea and then they got together and Heera said to Kalka, "Papa. We have planned to get you married to Ma this Sunday at the temple."

"Marriage? At this age? You all are mad. What will people say?"

"We don't care for what people say, but think of the happiness it will give Ma to be your lawfully wedded wife. Throughout her life she has not got this respect. Please Papa," pleaded Aina.

And Kalka agreed. They prepared to give Bijli a surprise.

Aina told her, "Ma, we will go to the temple on Sunday for a celebration. Many people will be there, so we all must wear very good clothes."

When Aina took out a red sari, Bijli showed her hesitation but on Kalka's insistence she wore it. Kalka led her to the temple and asked her to marry him. She was at first shocked and concerned about what society would say, but then Heera and Aina prevailed on her and she let herself be happy. She looked like a young, new, shy bride when the wedding rituals were done.

After the wedding, Bijli embraced Aina and said, "Thank you Aina. You have fulfilled my wish."

Aina replied, "I told you that you never know what life has in store for you. Be very happy, Ma."

CHAPTER 35

Rocoo finally got released from prison after serving his sentence. His immediate concern was to find Maakhan. Before he had been put into prison, all the people in his gang had decided where they would meet if they were separated or caught.

So the first thing that Rocoo did was to go to the Lucknow railway station. After several days of waiting, another gang member told him about the whereabouts of Maakhan. He finally located Maakhan. He was shocked to see the burnt face of Maakhan. They apprised each other about the developments in their lives.

Maakhan said, "That woman Aina, sweet talked me into eating food and then she started throwing the burning oil at me. That is how my face got so burnt. I wish I find out where she is, so that I can give it back to her. But though I have been to Rojpur and her parent's house in Najapur, I have not been able to locate her. I really want to torture her the way she tortured me."

They started discussing how to find Aina and take their revenge. He ordered for some snacks which the tea stall vendor brought wrapped in a newspaper. After finishing their snack Rocoo jumped up in delight as he stared at the crumpled newspaper. Maakhan thought that Rocoo had gone crazy but when he saw the picture in the newspaper, he also gave a yell of delight.

There in front of their eyes, was the photo of Heera and Aina receiving their award. The caption said, "Best Entrepeneur Award presented in Kanpur."

They read that the award had been given in the Merchant's Chamber. They wasted no time. They caught the first available bus to Kanpur.

Their first stop in Kanpur was in the Merchant's Chamber. Rocoo told Maakhan to stay outside and he went to the Receptionist and asked for the address of Heera. She refused to give him the address.

He pleaded with her and said, "I am in dire need of a job. Mr. Heera had promised he would give me a job, but I have lost his visiting card. Please give it to me or my family will die of starvation. I have three small children. How will I fend for them?"

And the Receptionist conceded to the extent of telling him that Heera's factory was in the Panki Estate. Rocoo was jubilant and with Maakhan he reached the Estate. They went around the Estate and it was on the third day that they located Heera's factory.

Both of them stood at a distance and watched the factory. Soon they saw a Mercedes car going inside the gate and Heera alighted. Heera looked smart and well to do in a suit and tie.

Rocoo said, "He has certainly done well for himself. He has got an imported car. I will go and talk to his driver and try and get the address of his house."

Rocoo talked to the driver Mohan, but Mohan refused to divulge any information. As Rocoo waited, another worker came out from the factory. Rocoo tried to speak to that worker. Mohan saw him and interrupted, "Why do you want to know about our master?"

"I want a job."

"Then ask him directly. Why are you asking us? He is a very nice gentleman. He might just give you a job. Come, I will take you to him," said Mohan.

Rocoo replied, "I am not well dressed. I will wear good clothes and then come to meet your master."

And Rocoo quickly walked away.

"Now how will we reach his wife?" asked Maakhan.

"We will have to follow his car."

But Mohan had not been fooled. As soon as he could, he went to Heera and said, "Someone was enquiring about your home address. He wanted a job. When I told him that I will introduce him to you, he made an excuse and rushed away."

"Where did he go?" asked Heera.

"He went and met another man who was tall and stout and had a burnt face," said Mohan.

Heera looked at Mohan and asked, "Can you describe the other man?"

"That man looked very dirty and bedraggled. That is why probably he said that he would wear better clothes and then come and meet you."

Suddenly there was a scream and they rushed to the storeroom where a worker was pointing at the window and shouting, "Ghost! Ghost!"

"What did you see?" asked Heera.

"A face. All burnt and horrible," answered the man.

Heera was about to run outside, but Mohan stopped him. Mohan said, "I won't let you go outside as they may hurt you. Let me see from the windows."

Heera called the security guard and asked, "Where is that man?"

"He has gone away."

175

"What did he look like?" asked Heera.

"He was a hefty man. His face was burnt."

"Why did you let that man inside?" asked Heera.

"Sir, he told me that you had called him for a job."

"Why did you believe him? I think I will have to change the security."

"Please Sir, forgive me. I will be more careful now."

Heera said, "Don't let any stranger come inside. Even if any person says that they have come to repair the phone or machines, don't let them come in. You must first check with me. Specially be careful of that burly man with a burnt face."

Heera sat in the car and ordered, "Drive the car towards the place where the two men met."

Mohan drove past that place but nobody was anywhere around. Heera tried to remain alert to check whether anyone was following him, but he couldn't see anyone. He thought, "Should I tell Aina? She is in danger as she goes to teach. She should know that someone is asking about us. The man with the burnt face can be Maakhan. The other man can be Rocoo."

Aina was really scared when Heera told her. They sat down and talked to Bijli, Kalka and Laila. Heera told them, "There is threat to all of us. Rocoo and Maakhan may try to harm us."

The family members debated whether they should tell Khushi and Prasan. They finally decided to tell them to stay away from strangers.

Heera said, "May be Rocoo and Maakhan don't know our home address, but as they have reached our factory, they may follow me and reach our house also."

They went all over the large house, closing the bolts. They looked outside but already it was dark and they couldn't see anyone. Aina forced Heera to call the police. He told the police about the danger to them from Rocoo and Maakhan. The next day Laila would not let anyone go outside till he had checked that it was safe.

He sat with the driver in the car with Aina and the children. They first took the children to their school. Aina talked to the Principal. She told her about the threat and told her not to send the children out with anyone except family members. Laila and Mohan went to leave Aina to the College where she was a Lecturer. Everywhere Laila and Mohan kept their eyes skinned for Rocoo and Maakhan, but they could not see anyone.

Meanwhile Heera called the police again, "I had lodged a complaint yesterday. My family and I are in danger, but you all have done nothing about it."

"See, we have a political rally in the city and we have to send all the extra police force in that. I cannot send anyone to guard you," was the brusque reply.

Heera then called his security guard and told him to get four watchmen for the house. He insisted that he would meet the four security guards before they were put on duty. Then Heera went to his factory.

When he was returning from the factory, he felt that a car was following him. He tried to see the people in the light green Fiat car, but couldn't. He told the driver, "Be alert. If anyone tries to stop us, don't stop."

"Sir, that car is definitely following us."

"Mohan, don't take any lonely stretch and try to shake off the car. I don't want them to see our house." Mohan started driving very fast and he took quick turns and soon they could not see the light green Fiat car that had been following them. They reached their house without mishap.

But when he told everyone this, Bijli said, "I can't take this tension. I keep worrying about you all. Do you know anyone in the police here in Kanpur?"

"I don't know anyone. I don't even know who is the Deputy Inspector General of the police here."

Laila said, "I know. He is some Verma who has just been transferred here."

Aina asked, "Could he be Inspector Verma whom we had met in the stadium?"

Heera answered, "May be, but I don't want to take anyone's obligation."

After that the subject was closed. The problem that came up was, that there was a Drill Display at the school of Khushi and Prasan and both were taking part, not only in the match past, but also in the class drill and the races. The children wanted that everyone from the family should attend the Drill Display.

Aina told Heera, "I am scared about all of us being at the Drill Display. It is for the public and anyone can enter. What if Rocoo and Maakhan come there?"

"I don't think that Rocoo and Maakhan can get into the spectator's stands because we have to carry a pass issued by the school."

"But they can stand outside and from there they can harm any of us. We shouldn't go."

"Yes, you are right Aina."

But the children did not agree. Khushi clinched it by saying, "It is my last Drill Display in school."

Khushi forced all of them to attend the Drill Display.

CHAPTER 36

All the family members were careful when they reached the school and got down from their car.

Heera told Mohan, "Keep alert and if you see those two men, inform me."

Aina spoke to Khushi and Prasan, "There are two men who want to harm us. One is short and fat, and the other is burly and has a burnt face. Keep away from them. There is nothing wrong if you run away from them. If you see them, come and tell us at once."

Aina, Heera, Laila and Bijli went and sat in the enclosure for parents. Both the children went to join their classmates and then the Chief Guest came. Happily Aina exclaimed, "It is Inspector Verma. What a co-incidence! We must meet him."

"No," said Heera, but Aina had already rushed towards Verma. She stood in front of him and folded her hands. Surprised, Verma looked at her. He said, "Madam. How are you? You look just the same."

Aina replied quickly, "And the situation is the same also. Rocoo is out of prison and Maakhan is in Kanpur and both are after us. We called the police but they said that there is a political rally and they can't spare their policemen to give us security."

"That is too bad. I will take them to task."

Till then, the reluctant Heera had also come down to meet Verma and they shook hands.

179

Verma said, "Give me your address and I will see to it that you get police protection."

Heera gave Verma his visiting card and soon, Aina and Heera had to move away because the Drill Display had started. It was a good day for Khushi and Prasan. They were excellent in the March Past and Drill, and they also won their class races.

But then there was a very interesting inter house competition in which Khushi was representing her Blue House. One student from every House was given a list of things to collect from the audience. As soon as the competition started, the audience started helping the children. Khushi started collecting the things. A five rupee note. A lace handkerchief. A printed scarf. A black pen. A spectacle case. An empty icecream cup. A lipstick. A red hairclip. A blue bangle and a grey hat.

Soon Khushi had collected nine of the things in the list. Only the grey hat was left because she could see a black hat and a white hat but she could not see a grey hat. And then in the last row she saw a grey hat.

She ran as fast as she could and she yelled, "Uncle, I need your hat. I will return it as soon as the race finishes. Please give me your hat Uncle."

The hat was taken off and then Khushi nearly screamed as she saw the burnt face of the man wearing that hat. The man tried to grab her hand. She quickly left the hat and ran straight to Heera and she whispered to him, "Papa, there is a man with a burnt face in the last row. He tried to grab my hand. He looks tall and hefty too. He must be the man you told us about."

She pointed out the place where she had seen the man. Immediately Heera ran behind, but that seat was unoccupied. He scanned the last row, but he could not see anyone with a burnt face. Khushi was standing near Heera and she said, "He is not here. He must have gone away. That dratted man! I was going to win the race. He spoilt it all."

"The race is still on. You go and finish the race, Khushi. I will keep a watch for that man."

Khushi ran around looking for another grey hat. She found it on the head of an old man and that kind man gave her the hat. She ran to the finishing line, but two other boys had reached before her. She could only come third in the race. She really regretted not winning the race after being so close to victory.

Aina wanted to tell Verma that the man with the burnt face was there, but Aina and Heera could not get close to Verma and after the Prize Distribution, Verma went away. Khushi and Prasan came and then they walked towards their car. Most of the cars had gone away and Mohan brought their car right to the portico. They sat in the car and Mohan drove swiftly away.

Heera asked, "The man with the burnt face is here. Mohan, did you see him or the other man?"

"Sir, I did not see them in school but now they are following us in that light green Fiat again."

Mohan drove cleverly and shook them off their tail again. As soon as they reached home, the two guards opened the gate and Mohan drove inside. By the time the guards shut the gate, they all dashed inside.

Just as Heera came in last, a gunshot whizzed past him, barely missing him. Heera shut the front door and so the next two gunshots did not reach them, but suddenly they heard more gunshots near the gate.

Mohan was still outside. He hid behind the car and shouted, "Guards. Shoot these people if they try to come in." They heard some more gunshots and then they heard the car drive away fast.

They were all very shaken by the incident and dinner was a solemn affair. Then Khushi asked, "Who are these people who were shooting at us? Papa, why did they shoot at you? What have you done?"

Heera explained, "I forget that you are a grown up fifteen year old in Senior Cambridge. I think I should tell you the facts. One of them is Rocoo and he was a spy. We got him into prison many years back. Your mother gave the evidence. Now he has come out from the prison. So I think he wants to take revenge from us."

"Who are the other people?" asked Prasan.

"There is just one more man whose name is Maakhan. When Rocoo was sent to prison, Maakhan came to kill your mother because he wanted to take revenge for his partner Rocoo. But Aina threw hot oil on his face and he got burnt," said Heera.

"Ma, how did you get the guts to do all this?"

His big eyes wide with surprise, Prasan also said, "My word! But you have been very brave."

Aina was far from feeling brave. She was terribly scared that Rocoo and Maakhan would harm her family.

She said, "Khushi and Prasan, you must stay alert. These people may try to get back at me by harming you both."

A look of fear crossed Khushi's face. Aina then said, "Always remember that if you get caught in a tight spot, it is normal to be afraid. Then you must take deep breaths and then think your way out of the situation. Those who have nerves of steel, are with the advantage that they think and find a way out."

"What did you feel at that time, Ma?" asked Khushi.

Aina replied, "I was very afraid. I actually felt panic, but I focused on my breathing and I calmed myself down and forced myself to think of a solution. So I could do all this. Tonight also I am feeling scared, but I am forcing myself to think clearly and logically. Being too emotional now will be the wrong thing to do. So I am not letting myself feel anything, except being practical."

Prasan said, "Papa, why don't you buy a gun? You can use it for your defence."

"You are right Prasan. I think that I will buy a revolver. It will be easier to carry with me in the car."

Just then the doorbell rang and all of them looked stricken with fear. The guard came and told them that some policemen had come to meet Heera. Laila and Heera went to meet the policemen outside and the police officer said, "I am Inspector Tandon. We have come here to leave two policemen for your security."

"Who has sent you?" asked Laila.

"The DIG police. Why did you have to tell DIG Verma? We would have given you security if you had called us directly."

"I did call the police directly, but I was refused security. Do you know? We are in dire danger. There was a shoot out just some time before. We could have been killed."

Heera told the details to Inspector Tandon about the shoot out. Heera also told them why Rocoo and Maakhan were looking for revenge.

The facts really sobered down Inspector Tandon and he said, "We will try and arrest Rocoo and Maakhan as soon as possible. Can you give me the car number?"

"There was mud on the number plate and so we could not see, but it is an old, light green Fiat car. It has a big dent on the bonnet as if someone hit it with a rod."

Heera talked to Tandon about buying a revolver and Tandon assured him that he would help him with all the formalities and also in selecting one.

The next day was a holiday for the children, Aina also took leave and stayed at home. When Heera went to his factory, a car with two policemen followed him. But though they kept a look out, they could not see a light green Fiat. When they were returning, Mohan said, "Just be careful, Sir. The policemen are behind us, but a blue Ambasador car is behind them. It has been there for quite some time."

"I noticed it Mohan, but the policemen in their white Fiat car are keeping us covered."

"Yes Sir. But the road ahead is lonely, so they might try and surprise us."

And that is what happened. There were some repairs going on in the parallel road. So perforce Mohan had to take the lonely road. As soon as they took the lonely stretch that they couldn't avoid, the traffic thinned down and the blue Ambassador speeded up, zoomed past them and stopped the car right across the road.

Heera got a quick look at Rocoo who was driving the car and the burnt face of Maakhan sitting near Rocoo. But the policemen were quick too. They zoomed right behind the blue Ambassador and put their white Fiat car between Heera's Mercedes and the blue

Ambassador. And then Mohan reversed the Mercedes as fast as he could.

As soon as Rocoo understood that the white Fiat was shielding Heera's car, he jammed at the accelerator, swirved the steering wheel as much as he could and drove away. The policemen also drove after them, but Rocoo turned the car into a service lane and the policemen lost the blue Ambassador. They then returned to Heera's house and they were relieved to see that Heera had reached there safely.

Heera was recounting what had happened to the family, when Inspector Tandon came in. They updated Tandon on the day's happenings.

"Where is Rocoo getting the money for the cars he is using?" asked Aina.

Tandon replied, "They are stolen cars. There was a complaint of theft for the light green Fiat at the Chunnigunj police station. Rocoo left the Fiat near the Reserve bank. We found it there today."

Heera asked, "What about the car they used today?"

Tandon said, "My people who were in the car behind you, had given me the number of the blue Ambassador and I found out that, it is also a stolen car. That is why it is proving difficult to nab them. But we are on the job. We will catch them very soon."

"What if they harm us before you catch them?" asked Khushi.

"Stay at home tomorrow. Don't go to school," said Tandon.

Khushi said vehemently, "No way. I will not be a coward. My mother was so brave in the past. I will not get frightened by two criminals. I will go to school."

Prasan also said, "I will go to school too and if they come near me, I will hit them hard with the hockey stick that I carry to school everyday."

"I must say that you both are very brave. I will try my best to catch both the ruffians soon," said Tandon.

But the family did not believe Tandon. He looked quite unlike a cop. He was short and fat and slovenly dressed. He did not inspire confidence that he would be able to do smart detective work. So the next day was also full of tension for Bijli. She saw off everyone and then told Kalka, "Isn't it very difficult to wait at home, not knowing what is happening, and dreading the worst?"

Kalka said, "It is. I feel so useless not being able to actively help the children out of this problem. I wish I could do something to get them out of this tension."

Just then the guard at the gate came in and asked, "Did you call for an electrician?"

Kalka looked at Bijli, who said, "No. We have not called for an electrician. Don't let him come in. Describe what he looks like."

The guard said, "He is short and fat. He says that Heera Sir had called him."

Bijli called Heera and asked him, "Did you call for an electrician?"

"No, Ma. Tell the guard to keep the man waiting. I am coming back. I would like to see who this electrician is," said Heera.

Heera told Mohan to drive back home, but the electrician did not wait. As soon as the guard told him to wait because Sir was coming, the electrician rushed away. Heera did not go to the factory that day.

He went inside and told Bijli, "That man might have been Rocoo. Ma, it is very good that you called me and confirmed, otherwise anything could have happened. We all need to be as alert as you have been."

Heera called Tandon and told him about the electrician. Tandon said, "You all are being very clever and alert, that is why they are not being successful in harming you all."

Heera replied, "But what are you doing?"

Tandon assured Heera that he was on the job and that he would certainly catch Rocoo and Maakhan.

Just then a call came. Heera picked up the receiver and the voice said, "Who is on the line?"

"I am Heera speaking. Who is calling, please?"

"I am the Principal speaking. One person had come to my office and he had told my assistant that he wanted to meet Khushi and Prasan. My assistant did not know that your wife had told me not to let the children meet strangers. She called Khushi and Prasan and the man has told them that their mother has met with a serious accident. Khushi and Prasan have told the man that they have to go to get their bags. Now Khushi and Prasan have come to me, so I am verifying this news."

"No, it is not correct. Please don't send the children with the man. If it is possible, please tell the peon to make the man wait. I am coming to the school at once," said Heera.

Heera told Mohan to drive fast to the school but when they reached, the man had gone.

Heera thanked the Principal for taking such good care of the children. Heera asked the Principal to give permission to Khushi and Prasan to go home. Then as they were driving home, Heera said, "Khushi and Prasan, I am very proud of you both. You have shown yourselves as very sensible children. That man could have kidnapped you. Can you describe that man?"

"He was short and fat."

"He could be Rocoo."

They picked up Aina from her College and then proceeded home. On the way they told Aina about the man who had come to the school. Aina was very quiet after that and when she was alone in their room, Aina said to Heera, "There is something more to all this. Rocoo and Maakhan would not go to such an extent just for revenge. Rocoo has just come out of prison and they would know by now that the police is helping us."

"How would they know?"

Aina said, "They must have seen the white Fiat car which saved you from them on the lonely stretch."

"They might be thinking that the car had security personnel employed by me."

"May be, but the fear would be there in Rocoo that he might be caught again. I am getting convinced in my mind that there is more to this than meets the eye. All this would not be done just for revenge, specially when Rocoo has been imprisoned for being a spy."

Understanding the gravity of the situation, Heera went and bought a revolver. He intended to carry it with him all the time. He would go to leave the children to school, drop Aina to College and then go to his factory. In that way, there would be more safety for everyone. Heera felt more secure.

CHAPTER 37

Heera said, "Aina, your ex-husband Daman Rai is in the news but for the wrong reasons. Read this."

She was now used to seeing the photograph of Daman Rai in the newspaper, as he had been made a minister in the State Assembly, but the item in the newspaper made Aina sit up in consternation. The headlines were in bold print. 'Minister accused of homosexual tendencies.' The article went on to accuse Daman Rai of being a homosexual and allegedly having an affair with a man called Manav. So the minister was being asked to resign from the cabinet.

Aina said, "What will Daman do now?"

The next day the newspaper brought a shock for Aina and Heera. An article read, "Minister clears his name.' Daman Rai denied allegations that he was a homosexual. He said that it was a conspiracy by the Opposition to malign him.

On being asked how he would prove that the accusations were false, Daman Rai said that it was a fact that people had witnessed that he had been married to Aina and had a daughter, but one day his wife had just left his home and disappeared with his daughter. He had tried to find them a lot, but he had not located them. Now he had put private detectives to find them out.

Aina just flopped down on the bed and she looked at Heera and said, "How will we face Khushi? That man has named me in the newspaper."

Heera said thoughtfully, "We will see to it that Khushi does not come to know. She doesn't read the newspaper and we will see to it that even accidentally, this newspaper doesn't reach her."

"Daman hasn't mentioned that I had left him for you, Heera."

Heera said, "May be because that would have hurt his prestige and ego."

Aina looked at Heera and said, "Do you think there is a connection between Daman and Maakhan? Daman told us that Maakhan was working for him."

"Aina, you may be right. Maakhan and Rocoo must be trying to kidnap Khushi, so that they can give her to Daman."

"But then why would they shoot at you?"

"Rocoo was a good shooter. Maybe he missed on purpose. May be it was just to frighten us."

"Then why did he try to stop your car?"

Heera said, "Perhaps to kidnap me and use me, to force you to give Khushi to them."

"That makes sense. It may also be that Daman wants you and me killed because both of us could tell the world that he is a homosexual."

"But Rocoo was angry with Daman Rai too. Why would he work for Daman?" asked Heera.

"Rocoo has just come out from prison. Daman might have given money to Rocoo as a bribe."

Heera said, "So it is possible that Daman, Rocoo and Maakhan are working together against us."

"Oh Heera! I am really scared now. I don't want to lose Khushi. It is a fact that Khushi was born when I was legally married to Daman Rai."

"But she is my daughter."

"But that would make her know that she is an illegitimate child that I had with you, when I was married to Daman. She will be shattered by this revelation."

Heera said, "Let us face things as they come. Don't let us anticipate trouble."

"But we need to discuss, so that we are prepared about what to do if and when the contingency comes up. We can't run away from this problem any more. Daman is a Minister. He has to maintain that he is of impeccable antecedents. He will not leave any stone unturned. He will try and prove that Khushi is his daughter. Oh! The very thought makes me terrified."

For once Heera had no assurance to give to Aina. Facts were such that they silenced him.

CHAPTER 38

Daman was using Rocoo and Maakhan. When Makhan had gone to Daman after his face was burnt, Daman had pretended that he did not know anything about Maakhan being Rocoo's man.

Rocoo had come one day to kill Daman. By that time the question of Daman's homosexuality had been brought up in public. Then Daman confronted Maakhan also of being Rocoo's man. Daman had told Rocoo and Maakhan that he would reward them if they kidnapped Khushi. Rocoo needed money and they agreed.

Daman gave them a part of the money decided upon, and he promised that he would give them a hefty sum when the work was completed. So with fervent zeal, Rocoo and Maakhan wanted to kidnap Khushi.

Inspector Tandon too had finally decided to take action. He had seen that Rocoo and Maakhan followed the children to school everyday. Next morning, Tandon told Mohan to keep to the road that he followed everyday. There was a reason for it. Inspector Tandon had laid a trap for Rocoo and Maakhan. On the way was a railway crossing that they could not avoid.

Tandon had taken a sanction from the higher authorities and they had allowed him to set his trap. They were to allow Heera's Mercedes to go and then quickly shut the gate of the railway crossing. When the car of Rocoo and Maakhan would have to stop at the railway crossing, the police would attack them.

That day when Mohan drove the Mercedes car to the school, to fetch Khushi and Prasan, he was sure that no car had followed him. But when Khushi and Prasan sat down in the car and Mohan started driving back, he saw two cars behind him. Both were white Ambassador cars. Mohan thought that one Ambassador belonged to the police, but it was not so. Rocoo was in first car and Maakhan was in the second car, because they planned to ambush the Mercedes from two sides. The time of action came. Tandon was standing near the gateman and the moment the Mercedes car crossed the railway tracks, he yelled, "Shut the gate."

When Tandon saw that the gate was taking too long and the Ambassador cars would drive through, he went on the fall back plan and yelled, "Jeeps."

Quickly four police jeeps jammed across the road, just before the railway gate. The Ambassadors had to screech to a halt. They narrowly missed hitting the jeeps. Within minutes, the Ambassador car drivers tried to reverse and then Tandon ordered that the police should open fire and hit the tyres of the Ambassador cars. Now that the cars were de-activated, Rocoo and the driver with him, had no option but to stay in their car because, if they got down from their car, they would be shot. So they started shooting at the police.

In the second Ambassador car, Maakhan and his driver started shooting too, but right in the beginning Maakhan understood that they were fighting a losing battle. So he quickly jumped out of the car and ran away. There was a pitched battle between Rocoo and the police, till Rocoo did not have too many bullets left.

Tandon could make out that Rocoo was trying to conserve his bullets, so he decided to play a waiting game, while his men kept shooting a volley of shots at regular intervals at the two cars. When there was complete silence from the two cars for some time, then the police converged on the cars. Some shots were fired from the first car, but the police men had protective gear.

After that, the driver of the first car came out with his hands up in surrender and said, "I am a taxi driver. These people forced me to come with them. I am not guilty of trying to hit the Mercedes. I don't have a gun."

The driver of the second car also made the claim that he was not guilty, but the police took them in custody. Suddenly Rocoo opened the car door and started running away. Tandon took aim and shot him on his leg, but just then Rocoo tripped and the shot hit his back. He fell down and the police arrested him. Tandon arranged to send Rocoo to a hospital. The police found out that Maakhan had escaped. By that time, Khushi and Prasan had reached home safely.

CHAPTER 39

At home Aina took care that no one could communicate with Khushi. She gave instructions to the servants, that if any phone calls came for Khushi, they should call her and not Khushi. She also told them that all the letters addressed to Khushi should be given to Aina and not Khushi. But the next day a girl in school came running and gave a letter to Khushi.

The girl said, "A man approached me in the lunch interval and asked me if I know you. Then he told me to give this letter to you."

Khushi opened the letter and was just about to read it, when the lunch interval got over and she had to go to class. The teacher came and after that Khushi got no time or opportunity to read the letter. Soon she forgot about the letter. In the car on the way home, she finally remembered the letter and took it out. She read.

My dearest Khushi,

You don't know me but actually I am your real father. Has your mother Aina told you that you were born when she was married to me? It was only later that she left me and got married to Heera and then she just took you away and disappeared. All these years I have been looking for you. Now that I have come to know that you are in Kanpur, I would like to see you. I would also like that you come and live with me. All these years your mother has denied me the happiness of having my daughter live with me. Think about it seriously. If you tell her, then your mother might allow you to meet me.

Aina and Heera have kept many truths from you. Do you know that Bijli, who Aina says is her mother, was once a prostitute? Do you know that Laila, whom Aina calls a brother, is an eunuch? You must believe me that you were born when Aina was married to me.

Your father, Daman Rai.

P.S. If you decide to meet me, call me on my telephone number given above.

Khushi felt numb after reading the letter. She felt as if the words were not sinking into her mind. She read the letter three times before the full import of the letter was absorbed by her. And then she felt a rage sweep over her. They had reached their house and Khushi stormed inside. She saw Aina sitting at the dining table and she stopped there.

Aina did not realize Khushi's state of mind. Aina said, "Ramu has made your favourite snacks. Freshen up and then come and eat, children."

"I will not listen to you. I will do what I want. You can call Prasan and feed him."

"What has happened to you?" asked Aina.

Then angrily Khushi burst out, "What a liar you are! You are my mother and yet you have lied to me all these years. I hate you."

Aina became defensive and asked, "What are you talking about? What lies have I told you?"

"That my real father is Daman Rai. You hid this fact from me."

Aina felt dismayed. So Daman somehow had got through to Khushi. Without realizing that she was indirectly admitting to the fact, she asked, "How did you come to know about it?"

"So, it is right. Why did you do this to me? Why did you keep me away from my real father?"

"Heera is your real father," said Aina firmly.

"He is not. Daman Rai is my real father. Here look at this."

Aina then threw the letter at Aina and stormed away to her bedroom. There her anger gave way to wracking sobs and she cried out the shock her system had been subjected to. Aina read the letter and then went to Khushi to console her, but Khushi wouldn't let Aina even touch her. Aina became afraid that Khushi might do something drastic because Khushi seemed really very upset. Aina called Heera on the phone and told him that Khushi had reacted very strongly to a letter sent by Daman Rai. When Khushi would not talk to Aina, Bijli and Laila went and tried to pacify her.

But Khushi yelled at them, "You both don't touch me. I know now that you were once a prostitute and you are an eunuch. You never told me about this. You all are such liars. My world has collapsed around me."

Khushi kept crying for a very long time. Heera came and he ran to Khushi's room, but Khushi shouted at him, "Go away. You are not my father. I was born to my mother when she was married to Daman Rai. He is my father."

After trying repeatedly to talk to Khushi, helplessly Aina, Laila, Bijli and Heera sat around the dining table. They were totally at a loss how to face Khushi. It hurt them that Khushi was so upset and that they could do nothing to console her.

Then they were surprised to see Prasan enter Khushi's room. All of twelve years old, they heard Prasan say to his fifteen year old sister Khushi, "Quit the hysterics, sis. Why are you creating such a ruckus?"

The family could hear what the siblings were talking. The very audacity of Prasan's reprimand made Khushi forget to cry. Khushi said to him defensively, "You can talk like this because you are so lucky. You are the real son of your parents, but do you know Prasan, my father is someone else. Ma has not told us the truth. She was married to Daman Rai when I was born."

Prasan replied, "What difference does that make, sis? You know that Papa and Ma both love you. Anything else should not matter."

"You are saying this because he is your real father."

"Sis, I would have said it even if it had happened to me. I can never doubt the love of our parents for me. Forget everything else and just remember how much they love us."

Suddenly Khushi became very quiet. Then she said, "Our grandmother was a prostitute."

Prasan replied, "So what? That was in the past. Today she is just our grandmother and she loves us. And now our grandparents are married. Imagine! How much she must have suffered in the past! I say that she is a very brave lady."

Khushi said bluntly, "Our maternal uncle is an eunuch."

"He was born that way. How can you blame him for that?"

"Why did Ma not tell me about it?"

"It is so simple. She did not want you hurt. She must have wanted to avoid this reaction from you. She must have known that you will dip into theatrics. And that is exactly what you are doing. She was sensible not telling us. We would not have understood all this when we were younger."

"Daman Rai wants to meet me. Should I agree to meet him?" asked Khushi, suddenly unsure about herself.

Prasan replied, "First you should find out why Ma left him. Something must be the reason. First you should talk to Ma and then you should take a decision. What if Daman Rai is not a good person? Come on, sis, snap out of it. Don't wallow in self pity. Go and talk to Ma and Nani." Prasan walked away leaving a very thoughtful Khushi behind.

Suddenly the door of her room opened and Khushi came and sat down near the family. She cleared her throat and said, "I want some answers. Nani, how did you become a prostitute?"

Bijli answered frankly, "My parents died and I had to stay with my mother's brother. They were very poor. He sold me to a man who took me away and made me a prostitute. And I must tell you one thing. Since the day I met your Nana, I have been true to him."

Laila spoke up, "Khushi, it is a fact that I am an eunuch. I have suffered a lot of humiliation because of it. I had long hair but I got a male haircut. I used to wear saris before, but I started wearing male clothes so that I would not embarass you all as you, Prasan, Aina, Heera, Papa and Ma are so dear to me. I love you all, so if I am a source of embarassment and you don't want me here, I will go very far away."

Tears sprang to Khushi's eyes and she hugged Laila and said, "No. You and Nani will not go anywhere. Let the world say what they will, you will remain with us."

Khushi also hugged Bijli and said, "I am sorry I was so rude to you Nani."

"Not at all, my child. You have grown up and you need to know about us. But I wish that you had not heard it from someone else in this way. It must have been a shock."

CHAPTER 40

Khushi said, "Ma, I want to talk to you alone."

Aina replied, "Ask me whatever you want. You can do it in front of the others because they know whatever happened in my life."

"Were you married to Daman Rai when you gave birth to me?"

"Yes, Khushi. But Heera is your father."

"You were not married to Papa when you gave birth to me."

"That is right."

"That means that I am an illegitimate child."

Everyone froze. No one had an answer. Khushi looked from one to another and then said, "Do you know what that makes me feel?"

Bijli replied, "Yes, you must be feeling horrible about it. But you should understand how all this happened. Don't be judgemental about your parents without knowing about the circumstances."

Khushi asked bitterly, "What exonerating circumstances can there be?"

Bijli said, "The fact that Aina suffered a lot in her childhood. Aina loved Kalka's wife Gomti like a mother, but Gomti was callous and cruel towards Aina. The happenings in the household while Aina was growing up were traumatic as was her marriage to Daman Rai."

Khushi said, "What will you say to the fact that Daman Rai was her husband but she was unfaithful to him and she had an affair with Papa?"

Heera became livid and he shouted, "Khushi. How dare you talk like this about your mother!"

Aina kept her hands on Heera's arm, trying to quieten him. Bijli said, "What I am going to say are the facts. Daman Rai was very cruel towards Aina. He and his mother Ram Katori really troubled Aina. Moreover, Aina never had a relationship with Daman Rai because he was gay."

"That doesn't absolve Ma from the fact that she had a roaring extra marital affair with Papa."

Heera shouted, "Aina, you don't have to hear these demeaning things." Heera got up angrily, caught Aina's hand and walked away with her to his room.

Bijli continued, "That roaring affair you are talking about was just once when they were together, when Daman Rai was sending Aina away from his house and Aina thought that she would never see Heera again. Khushi, imagine the suffering of Aina. She was treated cruelly by her mother and her mother-in-law. Her husband Daman Rai actually physically assaulted her. That made her vulnerable and so she showed weakness once. But she has never been ashamed of that one time, because she conceived you and you gave her a purpose to live."

"Nani, is Daman Rai really a cruel person?" asked Khushi.

"He actually kicked Aina's stomach when Aina was pregnant with you," replied Bijli.

"I don't believe you Nani. How can anyone do that intentionally? If he did, then it must be because he was hurt that Ma was pregnant through another man."

"It is your choice what to believe," said Bijli.

"Any man would be hurt if his wife had a baby with another man."

Bijli talked to Khushi for a long time. Khushi clammed up after that. She stopped crying, but she seemed to be introspecting upon her situation. She did not say anything to anyone, but when she was having breakfast the next day before going to school, she said to no one in particular, "I want to meet Daman Rai. Call him home on Sunday."

After the children had gone to school, Aina, Heera, Laila, Bijli and Kalka sat down to decide what to do. Aina did not want Khushi to meet Daman, but Heera said, "Let us call him, otherwise throughout our lives, there will be no end to this problem."

Kalka said, "What will happen if he comes? He will try to take away Khushi with him, just to prove that he is straight because she is his child."

Heera replied, "Then we can tell everyone the truth about Daman."

Laila said, "What if we don't call him?"

Bijli said, "Khushi will think that we kept her away from her father."

Aina said, "The main thing is what Khushi will decide. Would she like to go with Daman or stay here?"

That was the main thing that all of them were worried about. They were afraid that Khushi might leave them and decide to go with Daman Rai. The very thought made Aina cry. But Heera had made up his mind. Heera saw the telephone number of Daman Rai from the letter he had sent to Khushi and informed his secretary that Daman could meet Khushi at their house on Sunday at eleven. The secretary confirmed that Daman would come to their house on Sunday at eleven.

When Khushi returned from school, she did not talk to Heera or Aina but just asked, "Nani, has Daman Rai been contacted?"

Bijli replied, "Yes, he will be here at eleven on Sunday."

Chapter 41

Sunday at eleven a.m. saw the whole family nervous with tension about what would happen. At eleven sharp, the gate opened, and a car with a beacon light on top entered. Bijli, Laila, Aina and Heera remained inside. Only Kalka went out, as the servant ushered Daman Rai into the drawing room. The face of Daman looked the worse for wear. He looked more gaunt and his long nose stood out more prominently.

Kalka was as cold in his behaviour as Daman was. Kalka sat and just looked at him without speaking.

Daman said, "I have come here just to meet my daughter."

Kalka answered, "Then you have come to the wrong house, because your daughter does not live here, that is if you were able to have a daughter."

Daman reddened, but said, "I have come to meet Khushi."

Kalka asked Ramu to call Khushi. She walked in and stood looking at Daman Rai, who seemed suddenly uncomfortable, as if he did not know what to do. He said, "Hullo, Khushi."

Khushi only inclined her head, but said, "Ramu, go and call everyone here."

Surprised, Aina, Heera, Laila and Bijli walked into the drawing room and sat down on the sofa, without acknowledging Daman's presence. Khushi then said to Daman, "Say what you have to say."

Daman said, "First come here. I am your father."

"My father? Where were you all these days?" asked Khushi in a gentle voice.

The voice gave Daman confidence and he said, "Your mother had disappeared and all these years I was searching for her, but I couldn't find you both."

"Have you married again?" asked Khushi.

"No. I have not married again."

"Why? Is it because you loved my mother so much that you could not love any other woman?"

"In my family we don't believe in love marriages."

"Who all are there in your family?"

"My parents are dead and I have no siblings. So there is no one else in my house. That is why I feel very lonely. Come with me and stay in my house."

"Do you want me to stay with you because you are lonely or because of me?"

"Because I want to take care of you."

"Who will look after me?"

"I will employ as many servants as you want."

"Servants? I have a grandmother here, a grandfather, an uncle. They look after me with a lot of love. How will servants make up for that? Well, do you have the money to keep many servants? I am used to living in luxury."

"Yes, I am quite wealthy. You will live a luxurious life with me, more than you do here. Come with me without any doubts. I will be there to look after you."

"But you are a Minister. You must be very busy. How will you be there for me?"

"I will find the time to give you attention."

"But then how will you give attention to Manav? I think he is still with you."

Daman gaped. Then he controlled himself and said, "Who is Manav?"

"Your friend. He is your long time gay partner, who fleeces you of your money, isn't he?"

"How dare you? Oh! You must have read the newspaper. These accusations are all made by the Opposition to malign me. They want to spoil my political career and image."

"So where is Manav now, Mr. Daman Rai? Is he waiting for you at home?"

In a subdued voice, Daman replied, "No, some days back, when all the accusations against me started, that swine Manav ran away, after embezzling money from me."

"You deserve what you got."

Daman said, "But Khushi, now I am a different person. I have no one with me. I am utterly alone. I need you with me. I have waited so long to take you home to be with you."

"Is that so, or is it that you want to take me home as you want to prove to the world that you are not gay?"

"What rubbish are you speaking? Aina, is this the upbringing that you have given that she speaks such ridiculous things?"

Khushi said, "Yes, I speak ridiculous things. Do you still want to take me to live with you?"

"Yes, ofcourse. I will teach you how to be polite and cultured."

Khushi asked, "Are you cultured?"

Daman started getting really angry now. "Ofcourse I am."

"Is that why you kicked me when my mother was carrying me?"

Daman stammered as he said, "Your mother has told you lies."

And then Khushi said, "Mr. Daman Rai. Don't you dare say a word against my mother. Neither should you try to say anything against my father. Heera is my father, not you. Both Ma and Papa are the best."

"They were having an affair when Aina was married to me."

Khushi said, "That was the best thing that my parents did. Why should my mother have been loyal to a rogue like you, who could physically abuse her and kick an unborn child? They did the correct thing."

"I will give a better life to you. Come with me," said Daman desperately.

Khushi said, "You cannot match them however you may try. I am quite aware that you are asking me to stay with you because of your own reputation. I am quite sure that I will not go with you. I am not your daughter either. I am very proud of being the daughter of Heera and Aina. Now you can go."

A guard came running in and said to Heera, "Sir, this man has brought a photographer with him."

Daman said, "I want to take one photograph with Khushi. Just one photograph."

"How conniving you are! You want a photograph so that you can get it published in the newspapers that I am your daughter. Never. I will not have myself photographed with a person who has been cruel to my mother. You better go now, or I will get my guards to take you out."

Daman snarled angrily, "I will get back at you. You will be responsible for the repercussions of this. I am telling you that you will regret not listening to me. I give you two days to let me call a press conference to announce that you are my daughter. Think and give me a call. If you don't, you will regret it throughout your life."

"What will you do?" asked Khushi.

"I will get Heera into jail."

"My father Heera is a very honest man. He has never done anything wrong."

"I am the Labour Minister of this state. I can get your father Heera caught for any fabricated offence and I will see to it that it is an offence for which he has to rot in jail. Your eunuch uncle claims he is a big trade union leader, I will get him into prison too."

Khushi said, "Now you are being your real self. This is your culture. Thank God that you are not my father. And let me tell you, Mr. Daman Rai. If you trouble anyone in our family, I will call the newspaper people and give an interview in which I will speak of all the skeletons in your cupboard. So be careful, that you don't mess with us."

Then Daman Rai said, "Just act your age, you stupid girl. I can get anything done. Moreover people will believe me and not you. Just two more days or you will really regret it. Both Rocoo and Maakhan are sadistic criminals. And they love women."

"You tell your puppets Rocoo and Maakhan, to keep off us," said Khushi.

"I will tell them to keep off you for just two days. Today is the twelfth. On the fifteenth, I will call a press conference right here at eleven and you will tell the reporters that you are my daughter. That's it. You will do it if you don't want your family to suffer."

Khushi stood up to her full fifteen years of age dignity and replied, "I will not do it."

Daman Rai walked off in a huff. And as soon as he had gone, Khushi hugged Aina like a little baby, and said, "I am sorry, Ma, that I was rude to you. And Papa, I am sorry. Please forgive me both of you. I hope I did the right thing by talking to Daman Rai like this."

Heera also embraced her and said, "Ofcourse Khushi, you did the right thing. With any other person, I would have said that you went too far, but Daman deserved this, because he has really troubled Aina a lot. And please tell me, dear daughter Khushi. When did you become so grown up, that you defeated Daman Rai? When he went, he looked like a totally deflated balloon."

Laila added, "I would say that he looked like an utterly sucked out mango."

They all burst out laughing, relieving the tension that they had been feeling.

CHAPTER 42

Next morning, on the thirteenth, a letter arrived for Khushi. When she opened it, she saw a printed paper for questioning about money which the person was supposed to have embezzled. There was a blank in the space for the name of the addressee. On the fourteenth, another letter arrived for Khushi. It contained a show cause notice why the person had defied Sec. 144 by giving a speech in a meeting. There was a blank in the space for the name of the addressee again.

The family sat down and discussed the import of the two letters. They understood that this was Daman's way of letting them know that if Khushi did not agree to be called Daman's daughter, then Heera would be caught for embezzlement, and Laila would be caught for defying Sec. 144.

Kalka said, "Let us fight it out. Why should we get blackmailed by this blackguard?"

Khushi said, "He will get angry and hit back."

They talked together for a long time discussing all the pros and cons and were interrupted by a phone call. It was Daman's call. He wanted to talk to Khushi. Then he asked, "Are you ready for tomorrow? You have no option. I will trouble your family if you don't agree."

Khushi acted a bit. She sobbed and said, "Please don't hurt my family. I will do as you say."

"That is very sensible of you," said Daman.

And the fifteenth came and at ten thirty in the morning, Daman Rai came and the guards let him in. Ramu opened the door and Daman walked into the drawing room. No one stopped him.

Daman got Ramu to rearrange the furniture so that a sofa was in front and the other sofas were facing it. The newspaper reporters started coming and in fifteen minutes they were all seated in the drawing room. At ten fifty five, Daman told Ramu, "Call Khushi."

At eleven sharp Khushi walked into the drawing room. She went and sat in front of them on the lone sofa and Daman came and sat on the same sofa.

Daman said, "We have called you here to apprise you of the truth. This girl is Khushi. She was born to her mother Aina, who was married to me. Khushi is my daughter. If you don't believe me, you can ask her. She will tell you the truth."

One newspaper reporter said, "Where was she all this time? Where is your wife now?"

"Khushi's mother and I got divorced and then Khushi stayed with her mother."

Another newspaper reporter asked, "Are you really concerned about your daughter or are you doing all this just to remove the accusations against you?"

Anger whipped across Daman's face, but he said evenly, "I am really concerned about my daughter."

"Then why did you wait so long to acknowledge her?" asked another newspaper reporter.

"Her mother had disappeared with her. Finally I have found Khushi."

One reporter asked, "Can we meet Khushi's mother?"

"I think it will be enough to hear Khushi speak. Get up Khushi, tell them."

Khushi got up and said, "When I met Mr. Daman Rai for the first time, I told him that I was quite sure that I would not go with him and he said in reply . . ."

Suddenly Daman's angry voice filled the room. "I will get back at you."

Everyone looked at Daman, but he was quiet and quite aghast on listening to his own voice.

Agitatedly Daman got up muttering, "I should have known. They had taped my conversation. Where is the tape recorder? I must find it."

His taped voice spoke on in the room, "You will be responsible for the repercussions of this. I am telling you that you will regret not listening to me. I give you two days to let me call a press conference to announce that you are my daughter. Think and give me a call. If you don't, you will regret it throughout your life."

As the taped conversation went on, Daman frantically went around the room looking for the tape recorder, but he could not find it because Laila had kept it on top of the curtain pelmet.

The taped conversation finished and everyone looked at Daman. It seemed as if he was about to cry. Then rage swept his face and he shouted, "That is not my voice. This is a conspiracy to malign me. These people are not reliable. They have prejudiced my daughter against me."

Daman saw that no one believed him, so, humiliation written on his face, he just walked off, sat in his car and told the driver to take him home. After that, all the news reporters tried to ask Khushi questions, but Kalka came up and politely asked them to spare Khushi.

Inspector Tandon gave the news reporters the news that Rocoo had succumbed to his injuries in a hospital. Then the reporters walked out. Aina embraced Khushi and asked, "Are you all right? That must have been nerve racking. But you have been very brave."

Kalka commented, "Aina, it was a good idea of yours to tape the conversation of Daman and Khushi. It really did the trick. Daman was looking so frustrated, because he didn't know what to do."

Laila patted Khushi, but he was looking pensive as he said, "Heera, Rocoo is dead, but don't you think that Daman will get after us more now?"

Heera said, "If he does, he will prove himself to be very stupid, because after hearing the tape, all the newspaper reporters will know for sure, that if anything happens to us, then Daman would be the person responsible, after the threats he gave Khushi."

And the next morning, they saw that all the news reporters had reported the transcript of the conversation in the newspapers verbatim. Then, nearly everywhere, the topic of conversation revolved around Daman Rai, his gay tendencies, his coercion of Khushi and his cruel threat to Khushi and her family. And the next day he was reported to have been sacked from his post as Minister and even expelled from his political party.

Heera remarked, "Now his political career has ended."

Aina commented, "I wonder what he will do now. Will he try to get back the face he has lost or will he try and harm us with a greater vengeance?"

Khushi asked, "Ma, do you really think that he can think of harming us?"

Aina replied, "Khushi, that is no longer your problem, child. You have done your bit. Now you can forget everything and concentrate totally on your Senior Cambridge examinations." Khushi went to study.

When she was alone with Kalka, Bijli said, "A cornered cat always attacks. Daman must be feeling cornered just now. He must be cringing at the memory of all that happened in front of the news reporters."

Kalka said, "Now he has nothing more to lose except his wealth, as he has lost his prestige and status in society. And he told us that even his wealth had been embezzled by Manav. So he has lost everything. He is a dangerous man who will either harm us or harm himself."

Bijli seemed worried as she said, "At this very moment he might be planning to take revenge. I just hope that he does not target Khushi."

Kalka said, "I also think that we will need to be extra careful from now on. Daman is a very cold blooded dangerous man. I don't know what happened to me when I selected him to marry Aina. I feel so guilty about it and I really regret it."

"Kalka. don't blame yourself. Actually, it was the desperation to marry Aina early that forced you to choose Daman. No other proposals were coming. It was your wife Gomti who forced you to get Aina married."

"Bijli, I don't know why we all are in a hurry to marry off our daughters early. It is not right to think that marriage is the be-all and end-all for girls. Why can't girls have careers? Why can't they marry late or not marry at all? I made a bad choice in making Aina marry Daman, and see how she has suffered."

"Thank God, that Aina found Heera. I hope they remain happy and in love always."

"Bijli, we should pray, that our family stays safe and sound from now on also."

CHAPTER 43

On that very day, Maakhan phoned Daman to tell him that Rocoo had died. Daman was an embittered and desperate man and in that condition, he was not able to think rationally. Daman said, "Maakhan, you have to bring tragedy to this family. I don't care how you do it, but kill the lot of them."

"I read the newspaper. The blame will come on you if something happens to any member of that family."

"I don't care. Maakhan, I will give you as much money as you want, but just go and get that family. Even if you kill one member of the family, I will be satisfied. I want to make them cry."

Maakhan sat down at a tea stall and thought, "This is a nice opportunity to make some money. Killing just one member will do, but who should I kill? There is security at their house. It will be difficult to do anything there. The members of my team have all been killed or have run away, so I can't manage to get bombs to throw at their car. I have only got one gun. The best is to go to his factory and target Heera first."

He made a plan and then took the bus to Panki. When he reached the factory he saw that there were three guards at the gate under a supervisor guard. He kept a watch on the factory and realized that the time the morning shift of the guards changed, was the best time to get into the factory.

Next morning he saw the night guards yawning and handing over charge to the day guards. All the guards were near the gate. Maakhan swiftly went to the back and scaled the boundary wall. He ran across the open space and reached the back wall of the factory. He quickly tried all the windows in the back wall. None of the windows was open.

He saw the grill in a small window and realized that it must be the toilet window. There was a door just next to that window. He prised open the screws of the grill and then he put his hand in to open the bolt of the door near it. With a lot of straining, he reached the bolt and opened it. He was in a state of nervousness now because he knew that the guards would be coming anytime to take a round. One bolt still held the door.

Maakhan used his strength and pushed the door and soon had it open. He quickly entered through the door and he shut the door, just as he heard the stamping footsteps of a guard. He hoped he had not left any tell tale clues behind. He waited with baited breath, but the footsteps passed by. He realized that he was in the toilet and the door was bolted from outside.

Again he had to use a bit of force, before he could force open the door and step inside the factory. He became aware that anyone could see him as he was in the big Assembly Hall. He thanked his stars that there was no one in the factory. He dashed across the hall, looking for Heera's office. He knew it would be on the west side, so he tried the doors and finally he reached the office which had Heera's nameplate.

Thankful for the massive table that Heera used, he ducked under the table and sat down to wait. He was just in time, because it was time for the factory to start working. He heard the sounds of people coming, talking and finally being allocated their seats.

He got the fright of his life when a head came upside down under the table. It belonged to a peon who was dusting the edges of the table. It was difficult to make out who was more afraid. But then so many years of experience and training made Maakhan recover fast.

He grabbed the head, put his hand on his mouth and pulled the man under the table, saying threateningly, "Don't make a noise, or I will kill you."

He heard a car outside. He thought, "Damn, why did the peon have to come just now. I can't leave him or he will tell everyone. I have to keep him here."

Someone walked into the office wearing a very shining pair of shoes. "I will just shoot him," thought Maakhan," but just then, another shining pair of shoes walked in. "Which one is Heera?" thought the confused Maakhan. Suddenly the phone bell rang out loudly and Maakhan gave a start. Then he heard one of the men say, "Heera has not come yet. He is on his way. May be he is caught in a traffic jam. You can call after an hour."

"Drat it, how can I sit an hour holding this wriggling moron," thought Maakhan. The two men of the shining shoes conversed with each other and Maakhan could make out that they were Managers. One pair of shoes walked out of the office and one remained. Then Maakhan whispered to the peon, "Don't you dare make a sound. You can see that I have a gun. I will kill you."

Maakhan put the gun barrel on the peon's temple and the peon quietened down. They heard the sound of a car stopping after about five minutes and then quick steps of another pair of lovely shining shoes came into the room, with Heera's voice saying, "Amit, we have to send the consignment today. I am in a hurry. I am here only for half an hour because I have a meeting in the city. Where is Shankar? Hasn't he come today?"

"I had seen him some time back, but now I don't know where he is," answered Amit. By the increased wriggling of the peon, Maakhan understood that he was Shankar. Quickly Maakhan kept his revolver down and put his hand in his pocket. He took out a wad of rupees and gave it to Shankar and saw Shankar's shining eyes.

Heera's shoes came near his chair but they wouldn't stay still. They walked out as Heera went on an inspection of the factory. Ten minutes later he returned with Amit and finally Heera came and sat in his revolving chair, saying, "Amit, I only have fifteen minutes."

Amit walked away and then Heera seemed to be alone in the room and Maakhan knew that it was now or never. Maakhan pointed his gun towards Heera's chest and he pressed the trigger of his revolver. Exactly at that time, Heera swivelled in his big revolving chair and got up. The loud report of the shot made Heera take out his own revolver. Maakhan pushed Shankar away and stood up quickly. He pointed his revolver at Heera to press the trigger again, but Heera was too quick for him.

Maakhan fell down with a thud, dead.

Shankar was still under the table. As Heera looked at Maakhan falling down, Shankar came out surreptiously from under the table and crawled out and hid behind a carton. The workers and guards started crowding near the office, then Shankar straightened up and he ran out of the factory with the money that Maakhan had given him, thinking that he would never come back to this factory ever.

CHAPTER 44

Heera telephoned Aina's college and asked the Principal to let him talk to Aina. Then Heera told Aina about Maakhan. Aina said, "Heera, call the police."

"I called the police. They have arrested me."

Aina said, "Heera, I am coming to the factory."

By the time Aina reached the factory, Heera had been taken to the police station, but some policemen were still there. They did not allow her to go near the scene of the crime, but only allowed her to stand at one place and look at everything in the office. They let her photograph whatever she wanted from that position only.

With their permission, Aina took a round of the rest of the factory, inside, and even outside in the compound. She took photographs of the clues that she found there and made some notes. By that time, the policemen had finished their inspection and they locked the office so that no evidence could be tampered with.

Aina then went straight to meet Heera at the police station. She heard his version too.

He said, "I just heard a shot close to me as I was getting up, so I took out my revolver. Then I saw Maakhan standing in front of me with his gun pointed at me, so I just pressed the trigger and he fell down dead."

Aina then went to the court. By that time, Mohan had brought the children home and when he told them all that had happened, the family became very worried. Later when they came to know that Heera had been charged with murder, everyone started crying. But Aina did not cry because she had too much to do.

The hearing of the case began. Aina declared herself as the lawyer for the defense for Heera. The lawyer for the Prosecution was the wily N.T.Kohlu.

Kohlu accused Heera of calling Maakhan to his office and then shooting him. According to him only one shot was fired and that was from Heera's revolver.

Kohlu called many witnesses to testify. Aina was shocked that many of the workers of her factory testified under oath that they had heard just one shot. Four of her workers said that they had seen Maakhan going into the factory gate. These workers also said that they had also heard Maakhan and Heera having a loud argument after which they heard one shot. They said that after hearing the shot, when they ran to the office, they saw Heera with the murder weapon and Maakhan dead on the floor.

Kohlu also called Nathu, a new employee of Daman Rai who testified that Maakhan had lately been working for Daman Rai and Maakhan had been afraid for his life, because Heera had been threatening him.

Aina thought that she could prove many things wrong in the testimony, but she did not want to rake up anything about Daman Rai, because she did not want the past history to come up to hurt Khushi.

Much to her frustration, when Aina tried to rattle these witnesses, they held their ground. Aina said, "A bullet was fired from Maakhan's revolver. According to the report Maakhan's revolver had one empty cartridge."

Kohlu brought in a ballistic specialist who said, "Yes a bullet had been fired from this revolver but it was not fired on that day in the office. Maakhan must have drawn his revolver to defend himself from Heera, but he must have been shot before he could fire."

Kohlu concluded, "This is an open and shut case that Heera only can be the murderer. Witnesses heard him having an argument, they heard one shot and they saw him pointing his own revolver at Maakhan who lay dead. Heera should be punished with the death sentence, as without doubt, the act was a cold blooded murder with a premeditated intention to kill under Section 302 of the Indian Penal Code. The prosecution rests its case, milord."

Aina looked at Heera being taken away by the policemen and saw the droop of his shoulders. Her heart smote her because she felt that till then, all the testimony pointed to the fact that Heera was guilty.

Aina became convinced that Daman Rai was financially supporting this case against Heera, and he must have spent a lot of money to fabricate such lies, because she could not understand how the police and the Prosecution had managed to get such a strong case against Heera so quickly. Aina was surprised that there was no mention in the Prosecution case of the clues that she had seen. Later Laila told Aina that behind the courtroom, in the car park, he had seen Daman's employee Nathu, giving a lot of money to two witnesses.

When Aina started her defence, she called other factory workers and guards. The witnesses that she called to testify, said that they had not seen Maakhan coming in. She also brought out the point that there was no mention of Maakhan in the Security Registers. Kohlu started cross questioning them and many of her strong witnesses were made to contradict their statements, and were thus proved unreliable.

About the accusation that Heera had called Maakhan to his office and then shot him, Aina said that why would a person call a man to his office to shoot him. He would have called him elsewhere, so that people would not link him to the murder, but Kohlu objected that this was conjecture and she had no proof to rebutt it.

One security guard who on that day had been writing the names of the entrants, also testified that Maakhan had not entered through the factory gate. Aina then called the two managers who worked in her factory. They testified that they had not seen Maakhan coming into the factory. They also testified that on the day of the murder, Heera had been in a hurry to attend a meeting. So why would he call someone just to murder him?

Then Aina propounded her theory about what may have happened, supporting it with proof. Aina told the court that Maakhan must have scaled the wall and come in when the guards were busy at the gate during the change of guards. Then she proved that Maakhan had come from the back. She submitted photographs.

As proof, Aina pointed out the cans of left over whitewash distemper which were kept behind the back wall. The distemper had fallen on the ground too and she got it verified that the shoes that Maakhan wore, had white distemper on their soles. The white footprints were seen inside the factory too. They showed that Maakhan had come through the toilet, to the hall and to the office.

Under the office table too was the smudge of white footprints, showing that Maakhan had been crouching under the table for a long time. Then Aina called more witnesses, including the two managers, to testify to the fact that they had heard two shots. One shot was the bullet that had been fired from under the table at Heera. Aina said that Maakhan must have come in and hid under the table. He must have been crouching as he fired at Heera. The bullet must have missed Heera and got embedded in the wall behind Heera's table.

Kohlu said, "My learned friend should also give the court information about where the bullet is? The accused Heera is alive and uninjured, so the bullet did not hit him. Has the bullet disappeared into thin air?"

Everything now hinged on finding the bullet fired by Maakhan. Then Aina showed her photographs of the bullet embedded in the wall. As there was an open shelf which was affixed to the wall behind Heera's chair, the police had not been able to see the bullet in the wall.

The police were directed by the court to check the embedded bullet. The police found the bullet in the office, embedded in the wall between the open shelves, and this tilted the case in favour of Heera.

Aina went on to say that after Maakhan's shot, Heera had got up and Maakhan too had been ready to fire, but Maakhan could not fire another shot because Heera shot first and this second shot that hit Maakhan was fired by Heera to save himself.

Aina said, "This is a clear case of the deceased Maakhan coming stealthily with the intention of killing the accused Heera. He waited under the table and then shot a bullet at Heera, which went past the big revolving chair and hit the wall behind. Then Maakhan stood up and was about to kill Heera, when Heera fired in self defense. Maakhan could not fire a second shot at Heera because Heera's bullet got him first. But it was positive that Maakhan would have fired to kill Heera."

And then she called her last witness Shankar, who recounted whatever had happened on the fateful day. He testified to Maakhan shooting first and then standing up when the first shot missed Heera. He had seen Maakhan ready to fire straight at Heera.

Aina concluded, "So there was full danger of Maakhan killing Heera. Under Sec. 99 of the IPC the right to self defense should exonerate Heera from the charge of murder. So Heera should be freed from the murder charge. The Defence rests its case, milord."

Aina clinched the case and Heera was freed from the murder charge and the case was dismissed.

Heera embraced Aina, "You were excellent, my lovely Defence lawyer. Thank you so much."

Aina smiled, "I was being plain selfish. I cannot live without you, so I had to save you."

Heera embraced Aina and said, "How did you find out about Shankar?"

"On that day our manager Amit had seen Shankar in the morning, so I found it very strange that Shankar was nowhere around. So I told our driver Mohan to find out about Shankar."

"So Mohan has played a detective."

"Yes, Mohan went to Shankar's house and saw that it was locked. Then Mohan started contacting his friends. One of them told Mohan that Shankar was still in the city and that he was spending a lot of money. I suspected that Shankar might have been given money by Maakhan. Mohan finally found Shankar drunk in a new room that he had rented. Mohan forced Shanker to confess, telling him, that if he didn't, then he would be in great trouble. So he agreed to testify in court and that nailed the case and we won."

The next morning the news headlines screamed in bold letters that Heera had been absolved from the murder charge. There was another news too. Daman had died. He had been shot in his right temple. The news paper went on to reveal that investigations were on to verify whether it was a murder or a suicide. Later it was confirmed that Daman had committed suicide.

CHAPTER 45

And life went on. It had its ups and downs, but Aina and her family survived every problem with true honesty and grit. They did well in their lives also.

Heera became a successful and prosperous businessman. Aina excelled in her teaching and became a Principal of a college. Both started doing a lot of social welfare work. The love between Heera and Aina always remained strong. Later Laila became a mayor and that too in a sari, as Laila, and not Lalla Kumar.

Kalka and Bijli lived to a ripe old age and they played with their cute and loving great grandchildren. Khushi found her soulmate and the love of her life in her professional college when she was studying for her Management degree. After her marriage, she was blessed with one daughter and one son. Prasan became a fighter pilot and he married Lavanya, the daughter of Ranjit and Abha, and they were blessed with two sons. Ranjit and Abha were true to each other till the end

Usha and Sanad got their daughter married and lived with their adopted son and daughter-in-law.

And they all lived happily ever after.

Why ever not?

When amongst the family members, the need to be needed is fulfilled, then there is peace, genuine love, harmonious togetherness, contentment and good health which always give everlasting and sustaining happiness.

Happiness in life does not mean an absence of problems. Problems will be there, as they are naturally synonymous with life. Though Aina and the members of her family had problems, they also had the courage to face them in a unified manner, which stemmed from their love, commitment and dedication to each other, enough to see them with honest integrity through their exciting journey of life, right to their ultimate peaceful destination!